# Recreational Land Management

# Recreational Land Management

**C.W.N. MILES**
Professor of Land Management

**W. SEABROOKE**
Lecturer in Land Management

Department of Land Management and Development
University of Reading

LONDON
E. & F.N. SPON

First published 1977 by E. & F.N. Spon Limited,
11 New Fetter Lane, London EC4P 4EE

© 1977 C.W.N. Miles and W. Seabrooke

Typeset by C. Josée Utteridge of Red Lion Setters
and printed in Great Britain at the University Printing House, Cambridge

ISBN 0 419 11060 7

# Contents

# *Foreword*

*by* JOHN CRIPPS

*Chairman, Countryside Commission*

Active sportsmen find in the countryside the space they need on land and water, but much of the recreation there is informal and family-based. Whatever the degree of activity, access is often required to land already in other uses, producing food timber. To be successful multiple use requires skilful management. The attraction of the countryside for the visiting townsman also arises from the fact that it is managed in accordance with well-established rural practices.

The informality of the country walk or the motorist's picnic outing defeats the statistician comparing the popularity of various activities and measuring growth. It is highly probable, however, that informal countryside recreation outstrips all other out-of-home activities apart from social drinking and visits to friends and relatives. It outranks all sports combined. On an average summer weekend nearly three million trips are made to the countryside and stately homes of south-east England. Generally, recreational visits to the countryside may well have doubled in the past decade.

The rate of growth, the concentration of visitors in certain places and the fact that recreation may be only one of several uses have all contributed to the urgency and complexity of the resulting problems; and the processes of town and country planning alone cannot provide solutions. The problems are less of land use than of land management. In part their solution lies in that blend of information, suggestion and persuasion which goes by the name of visitor management, despite an apparent incongruity with relaxed enjoyment. It also requires the application of appropriate land management techniques, derived from rural practice, to the many acres of land acquired or appropriated in recent years for primarily recreational use.

Recreational land management can be regarded as a new and specialised component in the work of a long-established profession, of which Professor Miles is a distinguished member. He was one of the first to see the need for it. His collaborator, Mr W. Seabrooke is also a member of the university department which offered the first postgraduate course in their subject. They are to be congratulated on writing about it so comprehensively; and their practical approach will commend the book to entrepreneur, professional adviser, practitioner and student.

January 1977

# Preface

We hope that by producing this book we have fulfilled something of the need for writings on some of the problems inherent in the management of recreational land. Our approach is essentially towards the countryside and we have tried to look at the process from the inception of a project to its implementation. We are very much aware that there are fields which we have largely ignored which we believe lie in the minutiae of management. They are not, by that token, irrelevant but we were constrained to stop somewhere.

*Reading*
*March 1977*

C.W.N.M.
W.S.

## ACKNOWLEDGEMENTS

The authors wish to record their thanks for help, advice and information given to them by many friends and colleagues and in particular by Messrs Hamish Anderson, A.L. Bennett, P. Bennell, Colin Bonsey, J.C. Boston, P.D. Carter, Peter Cooper, M.S. Dawson, D. Gregory, R.A.H. Hearn, R.J.S. Hookway, W. Lanning, R.I. Maxwell, C.H. Moore, Major P.V. Moore, K.G. Robinson, Jeffrey Rowbotham, R.S. Stoddart, Michael L. Tebbutt, Andrew Thorburn, Alan Way, G.J.W. Wilkinson and Miss I.J. Clark.

Acknowledgement is also made to John Wiley & Sons, Inc., for permission to quote an extract from *Interpreting the Environment* by Professor Grant W. Sharpe. Thanks are also extended to Laurie Tomlinson for his permission to use his dissertation as submitted for the M.Sc. in Recreational Land Management Studies for the University of Reading in 1976.

CHAPTER ONE

# The Development of Recreation in the Countryside

During the twentieth century the demands of the industrialized countries of the world on their land and natural resources have increased more than over any other equivalent period. Where the land of an agrarian society is in the main required to supply food, timber and, to a limited extent, minerals, that of a predominantly urban society is called upon not only to supply such commodities, but is needed itself for urban, semi-urban and manufacturing uses and as a vehicle for carrying the greatly increased services required by the whole population. The satisfaction of these demands for land inexorably reduces the amount available and what is left becomes increasingly precious, valuable or costly depending upon who is assessing the measure. There are, moreover, additional demands, arising from the towns and cities, on that countryside which does remain while paradoxically the countryman himself becomes increasingly dependent on the towns for manufactured goods, services and entertainment. These varied demands generate competition among possible land uses and those uses which are identifiable are rarely substitutes for one another but are usually disparate, if not mutually exclusive, in nature.

Obviously the dominant uses of land in the countryside are agriculture and forestry, the former being both extensively and intensively applied, the latter, except where it forms part of a woodland nursery or of a manufacturing process (cf. sawmills) solely extensive. While 'agriculture' is a generic term it must be appreciated that it covers widely differing forms of trading activity and, looked at in this context, there are many types of agricultural activity which, as between each other, are basically different uses in themselves. The same cannot be said for forestry except so far as argument rages about the merits or demerits of a forestry use consisting solely of deciduous or coniferous trees. Thus farming and forestry might be said to contain a number of sub-uses on the worth of which the land economist/manager may well have to come to a judgment. This he, with or without further expert advice, is competent to do. By and large there is not usually much difficulty in choosing between the demands of farming or forestry so long as the financial returns of the one are markedly better than those of the other. As the gap between them narrows so the dichotomy of choice itself narrows; but usually not to a fine line except in the truly marginal hills and uplands where some uncertain predictions may in the end sway the decision. Where, however, other commercial uses are available and capable of implementation, the ultimate choice of use will depend not only upon the immediately predicted success of one over the other, but also upon the foreseen use which the land might be put to upon the conclusion of any particular project. Thus the choice (other things being equal, which they probably aren't) between arable farming and mineral extraction should not necessarily depend solely upon the profitability of one over the other in the short term but also upon what use is foreseen for the area when the minerals have been removed. In this sort of case a number of imponderables need to be added into the balance and although a 'result' may emerge at the conclusion of the exercise an element of highly subjective judgment is likely to tip the scales.

In other words, a choice of use must depend to an extent on the irrevocability of the use, or of the results of the use once the choice is made. An obvious example here is the decision whether or not to take land permanently out of all country uses and to develop it to an urban use. While countryside can reasonably easily be converted to town, town is not, in under several hundred or thousand years, reconverted to countryside; more, perhaps, the pity!

Therefore in deciding on a particular use reference must be made to the permanence of the use chosen, and the chooser must acknowledge that any decision incapable of being reversed once it has been implemented ought to be made with a sense of awareness for which the simpler changeable decision may not call.

This book is concerned with some aspects of the provision of recreation in the countryside, the first of which to be considered is indeed the place of recreational use in the queue of competing uses. It is all too easy to be emotional about this for, in the last analysis, the attitude of the decision-maker will depend largely upon what he does (i.e. why he is the decision-maker) and what he likes and dislikes and although precise calculations and arguments must bear weight that weight may be distributed differently by different people and for different reasons. Any argument, therefore, about the place of recreation as a validly competing use for the countryside must be undertaken subject to some achnowledged prejudice on the part both of the authors and the readers of this book.

If the need for recreation is justifiable the question then arises of the provision of sites for recreational use and of the facilities to go with them. In the participant's enjoyment of countryside recreation the primary element is probably the site and that, in the great majority of cases, will have been provided by somebody else (an exception does occur in the sporting traditions on many landed estates), namely by the landowner, public or private, who wishes to make it available for public recreation.

While over the last two centuries the pattern and balance of land-ownership has changed and the powers of local and central government over the control and implementation of land-use policies have extended, only comparatively recently has government, central and local, taken much interest in the provision of recreation in the countryside. In examining the manner in which policies for the provision of outdoor recreation have developed one must look at the nature of recreation, the environment within which it has grown and how facilities have been made, or have become, available.

The outdoor recreation movement had its origins in the urban areas of the industrial and manufacturing centres. Long working hours left little time for relaxation. Outings on rest-days were hampered by lack of transport. As a result, entertainment had to be sought largely within the confines of the urban areas, in the music-halls and cinemas of the times. Other forms of group entertainment — spectator sports in particular — rapidly gained popularity: but they also fostered the separation of participation from enjoyment.

The Factories Acts paved the way to improving the lot of the work force. Paid leisure time in the form of annual holidays meant that holidays away from home no longer remained the prerogative of the wealthy, though the tradition of 'wakes' weeks in the industrial areas of the Midlands and North maintained the emphasis on group recreation. Recreation became increasingly available outside the urban environment as the road and rail network expanded — mass transport increased and new forms of personal transport (the bicycle in particular) became widely available to the working population. As personal mobility increased a rising demand for outdoor recreation was coupled with an ever growing number of different sorts of recreation.

Although the past century has been a period of major urban expansion, even today the nature of urban development in Britain is such that the change from densely populated, intensively developed areas to sparsely populated countryside largely unencumbered by buildings frequently occurs over relatively short distances. Furthermore, not only can the town-dweller reach different surroundings relatively easily, but the variety of countryside to which he has access is very varied. Though his dependence on the town for work and shelter remains, for leisure and relaxation the dependence has become loosened. But while his affluence, mobility and leisure time allow him relatively free access to country areas in general, it may not necessarily be to any part of the countryside specifically of his choosing, nor one owned or occupied by somebody who is willing to grant access to it.

In the evolution of national policies directed to securing that part of the countryside available for uses other than agriculture, forestry or private leisure, little happened to disturb the *status quo* until the turn of the present century. The early 1900s saw some order being introduced into urban development and social and working conditions improving, and these changes paved the way for moves to preserve and safeguard a rural environment suffering the erosion of urban expansion. Mounting pressure for access to the countryside, particularly from the working-class movement, was largely and actively resisted by private landowners and their staff, the 'Battle of Kinder Scout' in the Peak District being one example of this conflict.

A significant change was introduced by the Law of Property Act 1925 (a far-reaching piece of legislation) which granted access to commons for air and exercise though leaving aside the matter of privately owned land. The Scott Report 1920 made extensive comment on the future use of rural land for agriculture and recreation, while in 1926 the Council for the Preservation of Rural England, destined to become an active and respected pressure group, was established. Partially as a result, no doubt, of the campaigning of the C.P.R.E. the Addison Report of 1929 recommended that the designation of outstanding areas of countryside for protection as National Parks should be investigated. Then in 1939 the Access to Mountains Act was seen as a further step towards greater accessibility to open countryside for recreation and relaxation.

However the Town and Country Planning Act 1947, which laid the foundation for modern town planning, omitted virtually anything other than superficial reference to the countryside, thereby losing the opportunity to consider the interdependence of town and country. The subsequent National Parks and Access to the Countryside Act 1949 was seen to represent the first outright statement of interest by the government in regard to the importance of safeguarding our rural heritage. The legislation lacked the political power of its 1947 forerunner, giving scant attention to how, in any plausible sense, policies could be effectively implemented. The relative lack of autonomy of all but one of the National Park Authorities subsequently established remains as continuing evidence of the uncorrected deficiencies of this early legislation. Additional support was given to the 1949 Act by the Countryside Act 1968 which established further guidelines for categorizing rural areas on the basis of outstanding characteristics, e.g. Areas of Outstanding Natural Beauty and Sites of Special Scientific Interest. It also led most importantly to the establishment of the Countryside Commission, which was given a major role as advisor, experimenter and counsellor in matters of recreation in and protection of the countryside. The Scottish Countryside Act and the subsequent Countryside Commission for Scotland dealt with similar matters in that country.

For the rural land manager this process of change heralds varied and greatly increased demands on rural land in addition to, and possibly in conflict with, the production-orientated rural land uses of farming and forestry. The management pressures in these fields have, for many years, been on increasing efficiency of production. Management has become less intuitive and objectives more explicit, often to the extent that primary objectives are adhered to with a single-mindedness which precludes subordinate or tangential objectives. This has brought criticism of farmers and foresters to the effect that their responsibility for enhancing and safeguarding the appearance of the countryside is being ignored in the interests of economic efficiency.

Today's land manager must know the total use-potential of the land at his disposal and the full spectrum of demands on that land in order to be aware of the factors which may or may not detract from his primary land-use objectives. The demand for outdoor recreation is one of these.

At this point the distinctions between concepts of public and private use must be clarified with reference to the use of facilities (which may incorporate land) and the use of land itself or, more correctly, the user-rights attaching to landownership or control:

(1) *Use of facilities* – implies the entitlement of recreation participants to use facilities on a normal contractual basis.

   (a) Public use presupposes that the public at large has, more or less, equal opportunity to gain access to the facilities in question which they are then at liberty to use. Ostensible discrimination exists only in the ability of potential participants to pay directly or indirectly to use those facilities. Facilities available to the general public may exist irrespective of the status of the actual landowner.

(b) Private use is synonymous with privileged use and presupposes specific individual rights of use excercised primarily on a selective basis by the controller of the facilities in question. Rights of use may be conveyed in numerous ways, for example, by invitation or by membership of an accepted organization. Again private use of facilities may occur irrespective of the status of the site owner. Needless to say the primary concern of this book is with the public use of facilities, although within both public and private land use.

(2) *Use of land* — as already mentioned may be viewed as a facility in itself, as in the case of a country park, or as a good, ancillary to other facilities such as, for example, a Safari Park. The matter of entitlement to the utilization of land for, say, the development of a site is more technical in a land management sense and constitutes, indeed, a specific area of land law concerned with estates and interests in land. The conditions upon which land may be exploited rest within the power of ownership to control. The freehold-owner of land has, to all intents and purposes, the ultimate power to exercise use-rights at his discretion. However he may, in a variety of ways, assign or subdivide his own rights to empower others to exploit 'his' land, usually to mutual advantage.

(a) Public use implies that the public sector controls the utilization of the site either through ownership of a legal interest, or possibly under some form of management agreement. Therefore, land in public use may be held, as a facility, for public or private enjoyment.

(b) Private use indicates that the use-rights of the site are privately owned, these rights stem from possession of a legal interest in the site which is held by a private individual or corporation. Enjoyment of the site may subsequently be, again, for public or private consumption.

The public sector has sought over the years to provide outdoor recreation facilities at national and local levels. The provision of Epping Forest for the enjoyment of Londoners represents an early and successful attempt to provide countryside for the recreational use of those living and working in an urban environment. It typifies the principle that supply should respond to the socio-economic concept of need rather than demand. Subject to predetermined objectives the identification of need may justify the provision of facilities, the extent and importance of need being reflected by the subsequent provision. Need tends to be expressed in terms of participation rates for readily identifiable, almost at times stereotyped, facilities.

The British Tourist Authority's Pilot National Recreation Survey 1967 points out that

there is no 'national' recreational man (or woman) whose use of leisure may be taken as typical for the country as a whole: in fact recreation appears to be one of these characteristics of our national population that varies profoundly on a regional scale. There is no stereotyped national pattern in our use of spare time, only a set of completely varying regional patterns, strongly idiosyncratic, and themselves probably composed of even more intricate sub-regional and local variations.

In short, the patterns of recreational activity in Britain are a mosaic of contrast, only quite local and therefore limited and restricted studies are likely to reveal its full detail:

aggregation to the scale of the 'Standard Regions' involves a first stage of general-isation with some loss of sharpness of focus: further aggregation of major regional contrasts to yield a single national pattern blurs the image still further; though clearly for many purposes the generalised national picture is the relevant one, and indeed a necessary frame of reference for more detailed analysis on a finer regional scale.

Further examination of the stereotyped nature of much public-sector provision leads to the suggestion that this is not through inherent lack of imagination (quite the contrary in many instances), but the practical implication of the judgment of the B.T.A. survey, that facilities actually provided, particularly for outdoor recreation, tend to be reduced to the most basic common denominators — often simply a 'natural' site and accessibility to it. The implications of this will be examined in due course, meanwhile consideration of the major suppliers of recreation facilities by the public sector will support this view. At a national level those who provide, one way or other, the opportunity and means to enjoy countryside recreation include:

(1) *National Parks* — First established as a result of the National Parks and Access to the Countryside Act 1949. Though bearing little relation to most international concepts of National Parks they were established to protect certain specific areas of especial beauty and interest where pressures for a variety of uses (including recreation) were great. The ownership structure within the parks was untouched and no additional public rights were at once created.

(2) *Forestry Commission* — Primarily established to promote and ensure the establishment of woodland for commercial timber production. Nevertheless, later years have seen a relaxation of the commercial timber

production as the sole criteria for achievement; greater emphasis being placed on the use of Forestry Commission property for leisure and recreation.

(3) *Nature Conservancy Council* — Entrusted with the role of managing and preserving sites of special ecological interest.

At regional and local level:

(1) *Local authorities* — provide facilities for outdoor recreation though often not readily identifiable, nor on a systematic basis. Provision tends to vary between authorities who see such statutory powers as do exist for the provision of recreation as an opportunity to be exploited, while others tend, through the relegation of recreation provision to the level of the non-essential, to ignore both demands for recreation and the exploitation of suitable resources. The negative argument sometimes put forward for conservative attitudes towards this type of social provision is that many of those who would benefit are likely not to live in the area.

(2) *Other providers* — these often do so as an incidental ancillary to another primary function, such as water collection and storage or gravel extraction. As often as not the particular operations generate a recreational resource, particularly where water is involved, which allows for subsequent exploitation.

Although in effect the response of private landowners to the demand for recreation may be similar to that of the public sector, the reasons influencing the ultimate result may be quite different. The demand of the population for recreation may simply be considered as a social and economic fact: where it is not exploited it is simply a phenomenon; where it is exploited it represents commercial potential. To this must be added the tradition on many private rural estates that accessibility should to some extent be granted to the public for the passive enjoyment of the amenity of a privileged inheritance.

A consideration of the provision of specific facilities for recreation and leisure must involve an active approach to the problem of the assessment of demand and of the subsequent investment necessary to exploit it. In doing this the private landowner meets problems similar to those associated with public-sector provision, but in addition a commercial organization faces problems which may not exist in the non-commercial approach, principally because of the different objectives of each.

In providing for outdoor recreation the public sector may initially take social provision to the point where only basic facilities are provided, leaving the users of the site to improvise in order to derive the specific enjoyment they seek. This level of provision has now come to be expected as a free good: it has also incidentally led to the criticism that these facilities cater for the higher socio-economic groups being those most able and willing to make use of these basic facilities. Although members of the general public are in certain circumstances prepared to pay to enjoy outdoor recreation, when they do so they look to receive more than they may believe they could expect elsewhere for nothing.

Commercial enterprises must, therefore, go beyond the provision of the most basic facilities (unless these are of a 'natural phenomenon' type, i.e. unique in character or occurrence) and provide facilities which leave less to the inventiveness of the participants. This, then, becomes less concerned with 'need' than with the economic concept of demand and all the management problems which it entails.

Reference was made earlier to the growing needs of the urban society to take and enjoy air and exercise in the countryside as a part of its normal life, and in the light of the greatly increased leisure time now available. There remains, however, the difficulty of finding out what sort of recreation in the countryside the majority of people want, mainly because both the questioner and those questioned do not know. The leisure-seekers want entertainment, something to engage themselves with, but the pursuit which is entertainment to some (e.g. walking) is torture to others and that which is diverting and stimulating to the latter (e.g. noise) ruins the enjoyment of the former. To ask 'Would you enjoy a lake with boating and fishing available?' is almost certainly to invite the answer 'Yes', but so might many another suggestion, the practicability of which in the circumstances may not have occurred to those questioned. When it is stated (as above) that recreation is one of the uses to which land may now be put, the statement is generally made in the abstract, for a recreational use may, like agriculture, be intensive or extensive, intrusive or hardly noticeable, so that the decision-maker may be required to decide upon not a general recreational use, but a specific one. In this context it is as well to be aware that many specific uses in the recreational field may have only a transitory attraction for the public (cf. the sudden and short popularity of ten-pin bowling alleys in the 1960s) and that in consequence the manager may have to consider not only the immediate attraction of his proposals, but also their long-term effect and the degree of permanence which they may carry. Here a distinction may be drawn between the intrusive and intensive fairground type of attraction and the true country park which may persist because, by its very nature, there is little specially artificial about it. If a piece of countryside is open to the public, the few specific amenities or services which it offers may be underused, or even ignored, almost without detriment to the present or the future.

Above it was pointed out that often an alternative active use is not apparent, that many uses are not fit and that a substitute for a particular use may well be no use at all. Either an area is farmed or abandoned (perhaps, however, forestry is always a possible use in place of farming, though farming is not always an alternative to forestry), but in so far as both are in effect 'natural' they may be classified as sub-uses of one major use. Among the choices other than farming, where there are any, that of recreation is not often made, for the constraints on recreational use are many and these are by no means predominantly statutory. Recreation is only a possibility where it is needed, not wherever it may be put. A country park in the middle of the Cambridgeshire fens is unlikely to be successful (for obvious reasons) and is therefore not a reliable competitor with fenland farming. However, the use as a country park of a small farm on the urban fringe may well prove not only very acceptable to the inhabitants of the town, but also a highly profitable venture. In this extreme example the problem of choice and the assessment of demand are reduced to virtually nothing for, in the first instance, there is clearly no demand to satisfy and, in the second, the demand for usable and interesting open-space recreation is virtually unlimited. In both these cases the assessment of the demand for recreation will be empiric. In situations where the answer is less obvious many will still consider that such assessment can only be based on observation and experiment, rather than on theoretic principles. The argument, if it starts, is always inconclusive for in fact theory and empiricism go hand in hand; the one probably stemming from the other. As far as countryside recreation is concerned, however, in either the public or the private sector, constraints exist before demand assessment can even begin. While the Countryside Act gives power to local authorities to acquire land for country parks most authorities will only consider using their powers of acquisition by agreement, and then only to acquire land which is likely to come on the market. For example, the buying of disused railway lines or of the traditional mansion house garden and park when such an area comes up for sale in the normal course of events. In the private sphere the owner suffers from similar constraints, namely, that he can only deal with what he has (and then only if it is available). It is not, therefore, often that anybody is really in a position to assess the demand for recreation which stems from a particular area, to decide where, as well as how, that can best be satisfied and then to provide it. The process usually works the other way round. Land becomes available at a particular time in a particular place — or emerges as from the mists of other uses — and he who can control its future is then forced to consider the uses to which it might be put, among which might be recreation in one form or another. At that point and in that place, he must then assess the potential or actual demand for such use. He looks outward from the point of supply, not outward from the point of demand. His searches and consideration are really little different, in the private sphere at any rate, from those undertaken by any entrepreneur, but are less easily resolved, for much information upon which to base a decision is still lacking in the sphere of demand assessment. The provision of recreation is not like the provision of one of the necessities of life. The consumption of recreation is highly elastic. People's habits change, their preferences change and their opportunities change. We may all need fresh air and exercise; we do not all like them and, while they may in fact be necessary to the maintenance and improvement of our mental and physical wellbeing, their consumption can be almost indefinitely delayed without any immediately apparent detriment. The urge to emerge from the artificial and crowded life of the city may, indeed, grow. One can safely say that countryside recreation will continue to be a need for the constricted townsman living a regulated life, but he can defer his satisfaction of that need in a way in which he cannot defer his satisfaction of the need to eat. Perhaps, in the context of countryside recreation, one should talk about a desire rather than a need in the first place, although, certainly in terms of mental health, need may be the more correct term in the long run.

In the public sector once a decision has been come to about the demand for recreation which a particular area will, or may, satisfy, it will then be necessary for the authority concerned to assess the cost and benefits to which the satisfaction of that demand are likely to give rise. Costs in this context are, of course, capital costs, both initial and recurrent, and revenue costs. At least these can be assessed with reasonable accuracy (a statement which must discount the impossibility of accuracy in times of severe inflation!). What of benefits? If the enterprise is to be run on a commercial basis with a view either to the realization of profits, or even with a view to covering the costs, then the benefits can be measured in cash terms easily enough, on the assumption that, if the venture successfully meets the criterion, benefits to users at the very least equate with charges they have shown themselves willing to pay to

acquire those benefits. Indeed, the instigators of the venture may, being
public-spiritied people, hope that the benefits received by the participators
may exceed what they have paid for them. Where little, or no, commercialism is involved in the venture, benefits are impossible to quantify
with any accuracy. In the short run the authority will have to persuade
its constituent members that the cost of the venture is 'worth it'. That,
in other words, the net cost is indeed balanced in the account by the net
benefit. Here there may be room to attempt to equate benefit with the
degree of use; an attempt which however can only be made once the
venture has been launched and the degree of use known. This presupposes some monitoring system so that the number of users can be
assessed with accuracy. But do we measure the use of Hyde Park? It is
acknowledged, however, that the majority of users of countryside
recreational activities are car-borne. It is easier to count cars than people,
and less obvious. Some authorities consider that it is right to charge at
the least for car-parking as a contribution towards the cost of maintaining that particular facility and to allow the general use of the recreational
element to be freely enjoyed thereafter. Many more may come to the
same conclusion. Through the employment of a car-park fee collecting
agency the first steps towards monitoring have been taken. However, one
comes up here against the first of the many financial problems, namely,
the cost of collecting the car-parking fees may exceed the revenue from
the fees collected. The point is mentioned again later.

Benefit may then be equated with the degree of use of the facility,
and it may be that one could construct a simple graph (or model) to set
the degree of use against the cost — both capital cost and revenue cost —
and thus to suggest that a successful non-fee-paying venture should, at a
minimum, give rise to so many visitors per annum per every £1000
capital invested and/or so many visitors per every £1000 annual cost.
The two tables would probably be better combined by adding to the
actual annual cost interest at an agreed rate on capital invested.

Where, however, no form of monitoring system can be employed,
the ultimate assessment of benefit can only be judged where public
approval or disapproval is provoked from those people who consider
that the venture is 'good' or 'too expensive'. The trouble with the
public's judgment, however, is that approval is often not expressed
where disapproval is made manifest by a vociferous minority.

As mentioned above the provision of land for recreation in the countryside has rather more facets in the private commercial sphere than in the
public sphere. In the first instance, of course, an assessment of the

demand for the facility is as important and as difficult. Indeed, it has already been suggested that an accurate assessment of demand in the private sphere is more important than in the public sphere, for an over-assessment of the use which the public will make of what is to be provided may result in the establishment of a loss-making enterprise, which may either have to be closed down or financed from another source of funds not designed to take on such a task. Revenue losses in the public sector, however, even if not budgeted for, will be financed out of public funds, and we are well aware that the general public often does not equate public money with 'real' money and hence is not as concerned about a local authority's losses as they would be about their own. Also the benefit argument can be used to justify a loss in the public sphere (provided the loss is both acknowledged and can be financed), whereas public benefit unintentionally conferred in the private sector often has to be paid for out of the proprietor's purse.

An explanation of the management function may, at this stage, provide the framework within which the problems of recreational land management may be further discussed. The management function is essentially a dynamic one, its object being the achievement of pre-determined objectives. In a general way, the process of management arises and develops in a similar manner for all enterprises:

(a) by the determination of goals or objectives, leading on to

(b) the preparation of a broad policy for achieving those objectives, and thus to

(c) policy formulation and the translation of policy into plans and programmes of operation.

The manager, then, has the responsibility of exercising direction and control over the implementation of his plans and the co-ordination of the resources at his disposal. Thereafter, monitoring, controlling and reviewing are continuing elements in maintaining the operation of management (Fig. 1).

The objectives of the owner of the enterprise form the foundation of the management strategy, hence the maintenance of socially acceptable standards may be considered a primary element in the implementation of policies and the internal efficiency of an enterprise secondary. Indeed, in organizations preoccupied with financial returns, this broader aspect of policy is sometimes ignored or forgotten.

It is important at this stage to clarify 'ownership'. In relation to recreational land management, invariably the primary resource is land

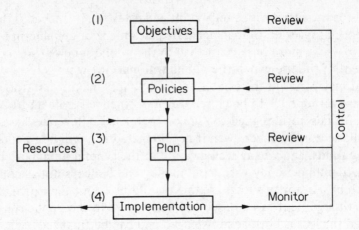

Fig. 1 The cycle of management

in one form or another. Under the English system of land tenure the owner of the freehold interest in land generally has, unless he has willingly assigned his rights to another, the ultimate power of use of that land. Total freedom of use may be restricted by legislation, but ultimately no other more positive land-use control effectively exists without the co-operation of the owner unless his rights have been usurped. Apart from this, statutory land-use control of a general or specific nature constitutes one of the management constraints within which the enterprise must function. If the effect of this control is such that it inhibits the management of the enterprise to a greater or lesser degree, the owner may comply with the conditions or may simply abandon the project. By the same token the continuity of ownership, or the lack of it, may have a significant effect on land management, particularly where this is based on long-term planning as it has so often been in the past. New owners may impose new objectives on management policies and plans with far-reaching effects.

In its guise as an organization 'management' may be seen as the nucleus of the system relating property-owners, workers and consumers. The links involved may be termed the fundamental relations of management (Fig. 2).

The manager must steer individual objectives within the enterprise (which will not necessarily be mutually compatible) to reflect the objectives for the whole enterprise. Probably the most difficult aspect in evaluating multiple objectives is assessing the weight to be given to each in the light of the whole. The land manager responsible for overall

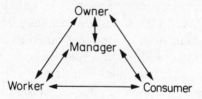

Fig. 2 Management relations

land-use strategies now faces an increasingly complex situation when it comes to establishing objectives.

In the case of rural land management the level of complexity which the manager is likely to face is normally dependent on the specific nature of the land uses in question. The more closely they are related to the generation of a tangible output — crops of one form or another — the simpler the task of establishing management objectives becomes.

Intangible benefits have, however, always been associated with rural land and frequently derive directly, rather than indirectly, from the land itself (e.g. amenity); but so far as the objectives of ownership and management in relation to these benefits are concerned, they are usually of a subjective or implicit nature. In this context the skills and techniques of production-orientated management are of little apparent application. There is no tangible commodity acting as an intermediate link between the land and the consumer of its produce. The consumer is, in a sense, now demanding the productive resources themselves. The link between producer and consumer via a market is gone — the consumption of the intangible benefits of rural land takes place on the land itself.

Land, by its very nature, is a non-homogeneous commodity (its location, if nothing else, makes it unique) and apparently similar sites cannot be perfect substitutes for each other. The owner is not faced, therefore, with a demand for simply 'recreation' or 'amenity', but with a demand associated with a particular site. He is not only concerned with an overall level of demand for a commodity but, more specifically, the proportion of potential demand that will direct itself (with or without encouragement) to his 'unique' site to obtain an intangible commodity.

The intangible nature of outdoor recreation as an output reintroduces the problems of establishing management objectives. The benefits, financial or otherwise, of countryside recreation to its recipients, the visitors, and to the owner of the land which provides it may be difficult to quantify. The temporary or permanent loss of resources, which may be thought of as a cost of production, may be equally difficult to measure. The benefit derived by visitors to a site may be ostensibly assessed by reference to the behaviour of the 'consumer' in response to the provision of the facilities and to the expertise of management. Although demand may be stimulated, such stimulation must be consistent with the objectives of the person or body to whom the manager is responsible. Consequently (although the extent to which expenditure on advertising or promoting a site is financially justifiable may be determined by the manager) the decision to spend will nevertheless be influenced by the objectives of the owner.

The land manager should be able to identify, systematically and objectively, the capacity of the resources for which he is responsible to accommodate or withstand recreational pressures. However, the decision to allocate land to a particular use or to a particular intensity of use and the establishment of the subsequent management policy implies value-judgments in relation to those resources. Value is the yardstick by which management effectiveness is measured: the value of benefits achieved are weighted against the value of resources employed. Management values are generally measured in conventionalized units primarily to facilitate comparison, and this is particularly so in regard to the resources employed in the productive process. However, the more unique the resources are the less readily can they be realistically measured by reference to standardized codes of value such as market value. In these circumstances the manager may have to resort to alternative values – the opportunity cost of the resources in question if deployed for some other use for which objective yardsticks are to be found (usually a financial estimation of market value) – to provide the decision-maker with information on which to base his decision. Ultimately the value which the owner places on his resources will be governed by his own perception of them. Although this will be influenced by the management advice given to him, again his own objectives may play an equally significant part in determining the value, and therefore the use, of resources. Indeed, it must be recognized that many of the attributes of land which are enjoyed for recreation today are a legacy from previous owners who adopted individualistic, often idiosyncratic views of the resources at their disposal and whose land was subsequently managed to reflect them.

The day of the individual owner of extensive country estates has been drawing to its close since the beginning of the twentieth century and there is no doubt that present social and fiscal measures are bound to hurry the end, but this is not to say that landownership as such will cease to exist (nor indeed that it can); it is a matter of the wider distribution of ownership interests among a number of people and bodies, of some substitution of the individual owner by the institutional owner (in many guises) and possibly by government or local government authorities. Such a dissipation of interests does not cause them to disappear, nor does it wipe out the responsibility of the corpus of those interests to provide opportunities for the proper enjoyment of the countryside by the population at large. It is, and will increasingly be, a matter of who is to exercise that particular responsibility of landownership. Where legal ownership and occupation rests in smaller units than formerly, the opportunity for the private individual to initiate a country recreational enterprise of any size will lessen, but this is not to say that the smaller, possibly more specialized (e.g. a farm or single subject museum) or more intensive enterprise will drop out of the picture. This being so, there is currently no reason to dismiss the private sector as being too small or irrelevant. In addition one may thankfully acknowledge that the private sector is still in being and that the historic house, garden and park, and the extensive area of privately owned agricultural estates are still available not solely for the individual's use, enjoyment and worry, but also for the pleasure and interest of the general public. Indeed, with financial pressures being what they are today a recreational enterprise, imaginatively and carefully run, may well be something that not only fulfils an owner's duty to the public, but also helps to provide funds for the upkeep of less viable portions of the estate and for the repair and improvement of the many farms, houses and buildings in the owner's care. Current tax law is such that rental income accruing from the ownership and administration of property is treated as investment income and subject therefore to the special tax surcharge applicable to that class of income, whereas the income derived from the running of a business, which a recreational enterprise may be, is not so classified and the tax treatment of it less severe. For this reason alone the active use of land by the proprietor as a business is well worth consideration. Furthermore, ancillary recreational use of a farm by the farmer may produce for him a much greater return than he can wrest from the land by growing crops or rearing or maintaining stock. (Hence the contention that a crop of caravans is better than a crop of corn.) Indeed, both the landowner and the farmer may find that a particular recreational use can be run alongside, or as a regular alternative for, another. The phenomenon of multiple use including recreation has yet to be more widely developed.

By and large, then, in the private sphere the recreational use of land will be established with the aim of its being a straightforward business venture designed for recreation and also for profit. It must, however, be appreciated that such an enterprise may well be fulfilling more than just the function of making a profit. If it is a success, it will be fulfilling a need or desire. Depending upon its type it may, of course, have set out to create the desire before fulfilling it, but, properly run, it may also meet the landowner's social obligation to make his land available for general enjoyment: the fact that by so doing he may make a profit does not denigrate his success in meeting his social obligations. He probably could not have undertaken, or run, the enterprise at a loss. However, there are occasions when a private country park may be knowingly run at a loss: for example, when it forms part of a much larger complex and can be provided as a social duty, or when its existence protects from overuse or trespass other more tender areas nearby. Indeed, the function of such an enterprise as a honey-pot may be of protective benefit not only to other enterprises in the same ownership (e.g. adjacent farms or young woodlands), but also to other enterprises or properties in other ownerships and other occupations. Often the proposal to open a country park may arouse bitter opposition from some local inhabitants who are at once and understandably afraid that their peace will be shattered by an influx of unwanted visitors, while at the same time the proposals may be welcomed by others who see the enterprise generating local employment. These sorts of reaction should be expected; indeed, they pinpoint some of the social responsibilities which already fall upon the multifarious owners of land, as indeed they fall upon most of us.

CHAPTER TWO

# *The Social and Legal Environment*

The unrestrained and unfragmented power of control bestowed on the owner of land and capital extends, in principle, over the management organization established to achieve the best use of those factors of production. This control may be imposed in a negative or preventative manner to constrain the power of management which, *in vacuo*, would be otherwise unrestricted. So the manager must operate within the framework of constraints imposed by the owner. Furthermore, the internal functioning of the organization may itself impose limitations on freedom of management, adding another facet to what may be termed the 'internal framework of management constraints'. However, management may be regarded as having a dual function; one internal to the particular organization, and the other which is essentially external to it. This latter function is represented by the multifarious relationships existing between the organization and the world at large. As an integral part of society the management organization cannot be immune to the social obligations and duties imposed upon it and owed to society in general (or individual members of society on whom its actions impinge directly).

This social interaction is external to the organization; it constitutes, in part, the external management environment and the controlling influence of this environment is exercised through what may be termed the 'external framework of management constraints'. The primary categories of external constraints are economic, legal and social/political, and although the framework which they create is always present, its form and detailed composition are continually changing. Some managers may convey the impression that knowledge of the internal environment of management is knowledge of management itself but awareness of the external environment within which management must function is a prerequisite for efficient and effective management. This chapter will consider some aspects of the external framework of constraints referred to: not the short-term constraints which arise from the flux of day to day commercial and social activity but constraints with the degree of permanence which common law and statute provide. The one notable exception to a definition of permanence is fiscal legislation, so much so that it is inappropriate to delve into this field in the present context.

The legal framework within which recreational land management functions may be divided into two parts: one is totally beyond the control or influence of the manager — such as the rules of common law — and the other operates essentially in response to positive action on the part of the manager — development control, for example. The relevance of the innumerable facets of the former will vary according to the precise details and circumstances of the management operations involved. The latter category presupposes a more specific bearing on the particular operations in question. Furthermore, the vastness of that part of the legal framework beyond the control of the manager limits consideration to those aspects which do, in fact, have particular relevance to recreational land management.

The law relating to the observance of an obligation between two or more parties is called the law of 'tort'. Tort consists of a wide spectrum of civil wrongs including negligence, assault, battery, trespass, nuisance and so on. Any act or omission constituting a tort may arise irrespective of any agreement not to do the wrong complained of. Although each class of tort has its own complexities (the literature on the subjects is extremely comprehensive), the law of tort is the source of two topics of particular relevance to recreational land management. These are 'negligence' and 'nuisance', and they form the foundation of the liability of the occupier of land or buildings for injury to third parties arising in particular from the common-law duty of care towards others. 'Third parties' in this context means visitors expressly or implicitly permitted to be on the premises, or others — including trespassers — who enter without express or implied permission. The meaning of 'occupier' is rather less precise but is largely dependent upon the degree of control exercised over the use of property and, in fact, there may be multiple occupiers of the same property. However, it is not unreasonable to surmise that when if the site manager cannot himself be defined as the occupier he may well be the agent of the occupier.

The liability to lawful visitors imposed on the occupier has been modified by statute — primarily the Occupiers Liability Act 1957. Section 2(2) of that Act defines the duty of care as 'a duty to take such care as in all the circumstances of the case is reasonable to see that the visitor will be reasonably safe in using the premises for the purposes of which he is permitted by the occupier to be there'. The occupier has, or should have, greater knowledge of the condition of the premises than others and should, therefore, be in the best position to guard against the dangers which may arise from them. Warning against possible dangers will only reduce the responsibility of the occupier if in all the circumstances that warning is effective enough to enable visitors taking reasonable care to avoid the danger. A person who in the normal course of events enters premises as a visitor but continues to parts of the premises where his entry is forbidden then becomes a trespasser. At this point it should be noted that the 1957 Act is not applicable to trespassers who may none the less rely on the common law for protection though the duty of care may be less onerous on the occupier than is otherwise the case. The occupier must have acted with total disregard for the existence of a trespasser before he is likely to have defaulted in what amounts to a humanitarian duty of care. It should also be noted that visitors entering property by virtue of the National Parks and Access to the Countryside Act 1949 are not 'visitors' within the scope of the 1957 Act and its common-law duty of care is not extended to them; so even though they may not be trespassers, the extent of the duty of care may be little more than that owed to a trespasser. A similar situation may also apply to the users of public or private rights of way although a long-established usage without objections from the occupier may give rise to an implied consent on his part for visitors to enter as they have been accustomed.

The degree of reasonableness in taking care to avoid danger will vary between classes of visitor and the circumstances under which they enter the premises. An adult, for example, may reasonably be assumed to guard against any risks reasonably inherent in his being there — an assumption which may not hold in the case of a child. Where visitors enter premises under a contract with the object of using those premises, the common duty of care may still apply in circumstances not covered by the contract; indeed, when the contract involves the transporting of visitors, then the duty of care is greater than may otherwise be the case. On the other hand, a member of the public entering public premises may be doing so as a licensee rather than invitee. In such cases the occupier does not owe the visitor the same duty to make the premises safe for his use although the occupier is bound to warn the visitor of any danger of which he is aware.

The occupier's liability to the general public outside his premises is practically restricted to use of the highway by the public. The source of this general liability is the tort of nuisance: he has a duty to prevent a public nuisance to users of the highway (including footpaths and bridle-ways) arising as a result of his occupancy. The essence of 'nuisance' is unreasonable conduct but in an action for nuisance the courts can take into account such considerations as the exclusiveness, continuity, in-tention and locality of the occurrence and the plaintiff's sensitivity to the interference. An action for private nuisance is known as a 'civil action' and is available to anyone holding an interest in land who has suffered particular injury not necessarily applicable to the public at large but peculiar to himself. Public nuisance, on the other hand, relates to an injury affecting a class of the general public and is not a civil but criminal wrong.

A nuisance arising specifically from statute is a statutory nuisance and may fall within the category either of public or private nuisance. Under Part III of the Public Health Act 1936 local authorities are obliged to discover the existence of 'statutory nuisances' in their areas and Section 92 of the Act lists a number of offences which are deemed to be statutory nuisances. If an authority is satisfied that a statutory nuisance does exist, it is obliged to abate the nuisance and this it may do by serving an abatement notice on the offender setting out the steps re-quired to stop the nuisance. In the event of non-compliance with an abatement notice a fine may be imposed or the authority may carry out the necessary work itself and recover the cost from the offender.

Any manager may be fully aware of the legal constraints which have been discussed and yet cannot be in total control of every action of the organization — ultimately day to day operations will be delegated to employees. The question of the liability of the manager, in the guise of occupier for the acts or omissions of his employees then arises. This is yet another facet of the law of tort but this time dealing with the res-ponsibility borne by a 'master' for torts committed by his 'servant' in the course of his or her employment. At one time the distinction between 'master' and 'servant' was pragmatically determined by the degree of control exercisable over a person as to the manner in which his work was to be done. In the light of the complex spectrum of modern employment relationships this has long been inadequate and the courts today may adopt many criteria in considering the existence of a master — servant relationship. The general rule when such a relationship does exist is that an employer will be responsible for the tortious acts or omissions commited by an employee in the course of his employment, i.e. within the class of acts he is employed to do or as a necessary incident to his employment.

The general burden of this liability can be constrasted, however, with that arising not from an employee, but an independent contractor employed for a specific, finite purpose. In general an employer will not be liable for the acts or omissions of an independent contractor committed in the course of the work he is employed to do. The position of concessionaires in this web of responsibilities may be unclear in any instance – particularly as exceptions to the general rules may prevent the employer from escaping liability. The issue to be borne in mind is not so much whether or not the employer is liable for a breach of duty on the part of the contractor, but whether or not he is in breach of his own duty. If the employer is also the occupier, he cannot shift his obligation of care by delegating it to a third party – he remains duty-bound to see that care is taken. Consequently where the occupier of facilities operated by a concessionaire invites visitors on to the premises, the occupier must take care to ensure the safety of these premises.

Finally, in considering legal constraints of a fairly general nature having more than superficial relevance to the recreational land manager, mention should be made of the Health and Safety at Work Act 1974. Its purpose is, in the words of the statute: 'For securing health, safety and welfare of persons at work, for protecting others against risks to health and safety in connection with activities of persons at work'. There is a specific duty imposed by Section 2 upon an employer to safeguard his employees while they are at work, but Section 3 imposes a wider duty which may have far-reaching consequences for the recreational land manager in that it extends not only to employees, but 'other persons'. Section 3 states that it is the 'duty of every employer to conduct his undertaking in such a way as to ensure so far as is reasonably practicable, that persons not in his employment who may be affected thereby are not thereby exposed to risks to their health or safety'. This is also reinforced by Section 4 under which the employer is obliged to ensure that others using the property are reasonably safe.

The responsibility for enforcing the Health and Safety Regulations is imposed, by Section 18, on local authorities. They need to be doubly careful, therefore, in regard to their own recreational establishments. It must also be borne in mind that in proceedings pursuant to a failure to comply with the requirements of the Act, under Section 40 'it shall be for the accused to prove that it was not reasonably practicable to do more than was in fact done to satisfy the duty or requirement or that there was no better practicable means than was in fact used to satisfy the duty or requirement'.

Although the code of law will shape future actions, its controlling function is, by definition, retrospective in operation. No matter how certain the site manager may be that he has taken such safeguards for the welfare of visitors, employees, third parties, etc. as could be reasonably expected of him, events may occur which are beyond his control or in the light of which the courts view his safeguards as inadequate. The penalties of such an outcome may be considerable and the site manager would be prudent in indemnifying his own liability through insurance of one from or another. The matter of indemnification is an extremely complex subject and, for the purposes of this text, it is sufficient to point out the wisdom of seeking expert advice on the question of insurance.

Having considered some of the more humanitarian constraints imposed by the common law on land managers, we now turn to another source of legal constraint – that arising from statute and embracing in particular the physical operation of the enterprise, i.e. the implementation of action to develop and use land and other resources for recreational purposes. The modern foundation of the general statutory framework controlling the use and development of land is the series of Town and Country Planning Acts, the latest of which appeared in 1972, and the ancillary legislation, mostly of a delegated nature, which surrounds them. The organization responsible for the administration of this control is centred on the Department of the Environment with detailed administration resting with local planning authorities who formulate policies for the development and other use of land in their areas. These local planning policies form a basic guide for subsequent decisions on more detailed proposals regarding land use and development.

Before land can be 'developed' in anyway planning permission in first required. This runs counter to the belief held by many users of, in particular, rural land that they have some latitude in this respect based on the assumption that an existing land use such as farming need not physically or economically preclude the adoption of some other use, e.g. camping, with little action on the part of the land user over and above this permitting it to occur. The definition of development embraces building, mining or other operations in, on, over or under land, or the making of any material change in the use of any buildings or other land. However, planning permission may be sought by one of two basic means, namely:

(1) Direct application to the local planning authority – this is the

most explicit method of which most people appear to be aware.

(2) Relying on a deemed consent under ministerial order such as the General Development Order 1973.

Hence many operations which are essential to the success of farming but which may be viewed as ancillary to *straight* acts of cultivation — for example, the erection of farm buildings — fall within the generic definition of development, but under normal circumstances benefit from a deemed consent, although in areas of high landscape value the planning authority should be notified of proposals which otherwise fall within the deemed consent provisions. Nevertheless it is important to note that permission for 'development' is governed by a statutory framework which from the land manager's point of view functions in response to a positive proposal from an applicant.

Development is not subject only to the controls imposed by the Town and Country Planning legislation. Obtaining planning permission may be just one of a number of statutory requirements involving licences and other consents designed to ensure that the development will conform to nationally and locally determined environmental and safety standards. For example, consent for the development of a caravan site may be followed by the need to obtain a site licence; signs or advertisements for the site must comply with the Advertisement Regulations; trees on the site may be protected from felling or lopping by Tree Preservation Orders; buildings on the site must conform to a variety of environmental standards often dependent on the specific use involved; new building work must conform to the Building Regulations; and not least of all access on to a public highway is governed, in particular, by the Highways Acts. It is impossible in this book to attempts a systematic unravelling of the multiplicity of statutory controls which can relate to recreational land use but the preceding illustrates the extent, if not depth, of the legislative morass into which the unwary manager may, all too innocently, step.

The discussion of the legal environment has narrowed down from the general code of common law through legislation having particular relevance to land management, even rural land management, until we have reached the point at which legislation becomes more specifically pertinent to land used for outdoor recreation. The forerunner of this specifically aimed legislation was the Access to Mountains Act 1939 which made an early and largely unsuccessful attempt at securing access (of a limited type) to open country which was almost exclusively under the ownership of private landowners. It was a further 10 years before this limited step towards freer access to the countryside was reinforced by the National Parks and Access to the Countryside Act 1949. As a result, for the first time, areas of Britain were designated National Parks with the objectives of conservation, enhancement of the landscape and improvement of facilities for enjoyment of the countryside.

The emphasis of the 1949 Act was very much national in character and although many of its provisions were strengthened by the Countryside Act 1968 the national emphasis was diluted in favour of a greater delegation of roles to local authorities. Notwithstanding this, the 1949 Act was subject to greater geographical limitation than the Countryside Act which as the name suggests had much greater general relevance. The 1968 Act revised but maintained the role of the National Parks Commission (established in 1949) which was retitled the Countryside Commission. The Act also granted new powers to local authorities. In particular they were empowered, subject to specific requirements, to provide facilities for camping, picnicing and outdoor recreation in general on either land or water. Nor are they restricted, save in providing camping and picnic sites, by the Act from providing facilities as they see fit — not necessarily in their own administrative areas.

In addition to the imposition upon all public landowning bodies to 'have regard to the desirability of conserving the natural beauty and amenity of the countryside', the Countryside Act 1968 extends the power of local authorities in regard to nature conservation, National Parks and access to open country. There flows from this a series of provisions which significantly influence the freedom of management of open land in certain instances. The first of these concerns the conversion of moor or heathland in National Parks to agricultural land if it has not been such during the preceding 20 years. This is prohibited without first notifying the local planning authority and receiving consent from them to proceed. Similarly restrictions may be imposed on freedom of management on sites of special scientific interest. The Act also contains fairly extensive provision for securing access agreements over open country, securing rights which could conceivably influence the management of land over which the agreement extends.

This very brief résumé of the legal environment within which recreational land management must function will give an indication of the breadth of relevant law, and having isolated one particularly pertinent aspect of statutory involvement in countryside recreation, follows through some of the general provisions of that legislation. The influence of legislation is not simply confined to this direct impact, and one of the most significant indirect influences on recreational land management centres on the increasing involvement of central and local government and statutory undertakers in the provision and management of facilities for outdoor recreation. In several instances their role is essentially that of instigating and implementing legislative proposals; the role of others has developed as a result of policy changes favouring greater involvement in recreational land management.

The focus of the public sector's involvement in recreational land management is central government; a surprisingly large number of its Ministries have some involvement in the field (for example, mountain-rescue materials are supplied by the Department of Health and Social Security through the National Health Service), although by far the greatest part is played by the Department of the Environment and the Ministry of Agriculture, Fisheries and Food. The interest of the Ministry of Agriculure follows two main avenues, the first through its advisory services and, second, by direct management involvement through the agency of the Forestry Commission. The increasing economic potential of outdoor recreation to the farming communities forms a path which many farmers are becoming increasingly interested in exploring with the aid of the Agricultural Advisory Services. Further impetus comes from the European Economic Community who are anxious that socio-economic advice should figure largely in the agricultural extension services of member nations. As far as the Forestry Commission is concerned Section 23(2) of the Countryside Act 1968 states: 'The Commissioners may, on any land placed at their disposal by the Ministry of Agriculture, Fisheries and Food or the Secretary of State for Wales, provide, or arrange for or assist in the provision of, tourist, recreational or sporting facilities and any equipment, facilities or works ancillary thereto', which makes the role of the Ministry in this case fairly explicit.

The Department of the Environment, as well as co-ordinating and controlling the planning function of local planning authorities and National Park Authorities oversees the operations of several other bodies with recreation interests, which include the Countryside Commission, the Sports Council, the Nature Conservancy Council, the National Water Council, the Water Space Amenity Commission, the British Waterways Board and the Inland Waterways Amenity Advisory Commission. The spectrum of interest encompassed in this list is broad but often of only specific relevance, so further discussion is limited to those with more general application to the field, namely local authorities, National Park Authorities and the Countryside Commission.

# CHAPTER THREE

# The Countryside Commission

## The Countryside Act 1968

set out to enlarge the functions of the Commission established under the National Parks and Access to the Countryside Act 1949, to confer new powers on local authorities and other bodies for the conservation and enhancement of natural beauty and for the benefit of those resorting to the countryside and to make other provisions for the matters dealt with in the Act of 1949 and generally as respects the countryside, and to amend the law about trees and woodlands and footpaths and bridleways, and other public paths.

Maybe it was in 1968 that Britain began to rediscover the country through the medium of this Act; certainly it brought many matters into focus which had been growing blurred. It gave statutory recognition to the fact that the population as a whole had a need to enjoy the fresh air and freedom of the countryside and it provided opportunities for it to do so. It also acknowledged that there was a growing demand for recreation which could not be satisfied solely by the private sector.

The National Parks Commission became the Countryside Commission upon which body many new functions were conferred which were 'to be exercised for the conservation and enhancement of the natural beauty and amenity of the countryside'. Furthermore, those functions were also to be exercised to encourage 'the provision and improvement of facilities for the enjoyment of the countryside'.* The functions of the Commission to be exercised with these aims in view are described in Section 2 of the Act.

Briefly they are to encourage and help in the implementation of proposals and to advise Ministers and public bodies on 'matters relating

* Section 1(2)

28

to the Countryside'. The Commission is further enjoined to give advice on special problems relating to countryside recreation or on matters concerning the enhancement or conservation of the natural beauty and amenity of the countryside. In carrying out these provisions the Commission can, and does, engage in research and investigation and provides interpretation and information services. Essentially the Commission was established as a body which has a function to encourage other people or bodies to act and to give them help and advice on the matters which it has a responsibility to keep under review. In order to be able to do this the Commission has initiated and commissioned research into a number of theses connected with recreation provision and with the conservation of the countryside. It has also, as it is empowered to do under Section 4 of the Act, set up experimental projects designed to help the enjoyment of the countryside or to enhance its natural beauty (cf. the Goyt Valley traffic experiment). In such cases the Commission acts after consultation with the local authorities and other bodies concerned and after the specific approval of the Minister.

In order to carry out these functions the Commission is given powers in the Act with the approval of the Minister to acquire land by agreement or, with his specific authorization in a particular case, compulsorily. This section is so worded that it is clear the intention is that such authorization will only be given in special cases; beyond this the Commission is empowered to hold and manage land, to erect and maintain buildings and equipment and to dispose of land, facilities and services.

Since the main duty of the Commission, as statutorily defined and as executed in practice, has been to encourage and help other people and bodies to provide recreational facilities in the countryside, as well as to be concerned with the conservation and enhancement of its natural beauty, it has not acquired land for itself. It sees its responsibility to experiment, research and warn more easily implemented not by its being engaged in day to day management, but through the medium of commissioned works and projects carried out on other people's land and with their help. Where this is done, money is provided by the Commission to run an experiment where appropriate (cf. the bicycle-hiring experiment in Clumber Park, Nottingham). Furthermore the Commission is empowered, in Section 5 of the Countryside Act, to give financial assistance by way of grant or loan to any person, other than a public body (and the National Trust is specifically not a public body for the purposes of this exclusion), for the carrying on of any project approved by the Minister which in his opinion is conducive to the attainments of the purposes for which the Commission was established either under the National Parks and Access to the Countryside Act 1949 or the Countryside Act 1968.

The Countryside Act (Section 5(2)) provides that the maximum rate of grant shall be 75 per cent of the expenditure concerned. There is no maximum rate of loan. As far as the grants to other than public bodies are concerned the Commission, in accordance with its powers, imposes certain conditions after full consultation with the recipient. For example, the Commission may impose a limit on the admission charges made for entry to a country park which has been established with the help of a grant. However, in every case the Commission seeks to agree a charge which should be enough to enable the owner to cover running costs and to obtain thereafter a reasonable profit on his own investment and this will be done on the basis of the agreed prediction of the numbers of the paying public who are likely to seek admission. If the predictions are wrong, or if some unforeseen contingency arises after the charges have been fixed, then the Commission states that it is always ready to discuss the matter again. The recipient is, of course, free to approach the Commission with a view to negotiating a repayment of the grant, or a portion of it, should he wish to be freed from any restriction imposed by the Commission on his enterprise. While the Commission does not normally set any limit to the period over which conditions attached to a grant remain operative it may be willing, in any given case, to negotiate a repayment of the grant and a lifting of conditions as if an amortization period were in existence. Naturally each application will be the subject of individual negotiation and will be considered in the light of any special repayment conditions which may have been imposed when the grant was approved. If a facility, towards the establishment of which a grant has been made, closes down the Commission may look to being repaid at any rate a proportion of the grant, the amount of which will depend on how long the facility has in fact been run. The facilities, the provision of which may be grant-aided through the Commission, are restricted to those which are essentially not of the 'fairground' type and would include roads, car parks, lavatories, information centres and the like.

Where a private owner negotiates to repay a grant because he thinks that the venture would be more profitable if the Commission's restrictions were lifted, there is no reason to query the reasonableness of those restrictions. It should be remembered that without any grant in the first place the project, however profitable now, would probably never have been started.

The special work which the Commission does with the voluntary bodies needs emphasis. It is currently developing a structure grant to the voluntary movement. The Commission, for example, has become the major source of grant aid from public funds to the National Trust.

In the public sphere the Countryside Act empowered the Minister to make Exchequer grants available to local authorities in respect of expenditure incurred by them on the acquisition of land for a country park, on the carrying out of works in a country park, in connection with litter collection or disposal and generally on the provisions of various facilities in the countryside (Sections 33 and 34). The Minister is required to arrange for the Countryside Commission to make recommendations to him on the making of grants to public bodies and to consult the Commission if he is contemplating making a grant where no recommendation has first been made to him by the Commission. However, the Local Government Act 1974 provided for the termination of a number of grants which had been payable to local authorities towards their expenditure on certain services and projects in the countryside and instead incorporated this sort of expenditure in sums accepted for rate support grant together with the payment of a supplementary grant for estimated expenditure connected with National Parks. The 1974 Act, in Section 9, provided that the Countryside Commission might give financial assistance by way of grant or loan to any person (including a public body) in respect of expenditure incurred by him in doing anything which in the opinion of the Commission is conductive to the attainments of the provisions of the Countryside Act 1968 or the National Parks and Access to the Countryside Act 1949. In making such grants and loans under the 1974 Act, the Commission is able to attach conditions to its grants or loans, specifically including the repayment of grants in special circumstances. The exercise by the Countryside Commission of its powers are here subject to directives by the Secretary of State.

The provisions of this section are stated to have effect in place of the provisions of Section 5 of the Countryside Act 1968, to which reference has been made above, and effectively give the Countryside Commission more autonomous power for (provided it acts within the directives of the Secretary of State) it may make its own decisions on projects to which it will give assistance without having to obtain the approval of the Minister on each project.

In 1974 the Commission issued a pamphlet (CCP 78) about grants which are available to local authorities and other bodies for conservation and recreation in the countryside and set out in it the projects, services

or other activities provided by local authorities which the Commission is
prepared to consider for assistance. The list includes a general assessment
by the Commission of the relative priority of the works in accordance
with their location, e.g. picnic sites in Green Belts are given a high priority
whereas traffic management schemes elsewhere than on Heritage Coasts
are rated as of medium to low priority. It must be appreciated that over
the years the relative priority of schemes is likely to change. Grants
approved by the Commission to local authorities are currently limited by
the Commission to 50 per cent of the approved expenditure because
much of the eligible expenditure may now be included in sums accepted
for rate support grant and thus to an extent fianced by the Exchequer
already (see above).

In all cases where grant aid has been sought the Commission will
consider how far the proposals fit in with local and structure plans and
how far they are compatible with the Commission's other duties to
secure the conservation and enhancement of the beauty of the countryside. Understandably the Commission seeks to be consulted as soon as
possible on any proposals on which they will subsequently be asked to
give grant or loan aid. Indeed in both the public and the private spheres
the Commission insists on full plans of the proposals being discussed
with them (including layout plans, ideas of the use-intentions of the
promoter and of his management proposals) before any commitment on
aid will be given.

While the private individual, and possibly some local authorities also,
may consider that the approval of their schemes for grant aid is a prime
function of the Countryside Commission, the Commission itself, its
officers and staff, consider that their major function is the giving of
advice on countryside conservation and recreation and on the reconcilia-
tion of these functions with each other. Indeed in these matters, with its
Scottish counterpart, the Commission aims to lead. It has already experi-
mented, probed and learned to a degree which should enable it not merel
to be in the forefront of the countryside recreational field, but indeed
to have ideas and practical knowledge in some spheres well ahead of
those persons and authorities who are actually providing recreational
facilities in Britain. Already several of its commissioned experiments
have broken new ground, if not in the world at least in Europe, and it
looks to being among the world leaders in the provision of countryside
recreation and in matters pertaining to the conservation and enhancemen
of the countryside. The Commission has been both wise and fortunate in
avoiding the temptation to engage in the day to day business of running

its own country parks. Little so effectively precludes initiation, experiment and research than a concern with everyday practicalities. The Commission's research aims are pragmatic and to achieve them it employs directors of research, rather than the researchers themselves, who oversee a number of projects which are 'farmed out' to a wide variety of interested institutions and individuals. Some of the results of the approved research projects are positive and others negative, yet even in that they have usefully proved that a particular thesis is untenable. Projects for research do not emanate solely from the staff of the Commission; many are put up from a number of different sources. Each project as submitted is evaluated by the Commission's staff and, if thought acceptable, is further evaluated by the Countryside Recreation Research Advisory Group (C.R.R.A.G.) which is a body serviced by the Commission through the medium of one of their full-time officers, and composed of those agencies who have powers to carry out research into aspects of countryside recreation in England, Wales and Scotland.

As far as specific experiments are concerned the Commission has powers to initiate these and to finance and monitor them, but they are usually carried out on the ground by the authority concerned: where special equipment is needed this is normally supplied by the Commission.

The Commission's research and advisory work and the experimental schemes which it is able to sponsor are having a major effect on the maintenance and conservation of the countryside. They are indeed beneficially influencing the attitude of the public and governmental and local authorities towards the protection of rural landscapes and towards the use of specific areas for public recreation and enjoyment. It was, for example, the Commission's study of the coastline that gave rise to designation of Heritage Coasts.

In addition the Commission is especially concerned with providing, and encouraging others to provide, information about the countryside both through the medium of special information centres and guided or self-guided walks and through provision of farm and forest open-days. Various interpretation and information experiments have been sponsored and the reopening or extension of rural railway routes financed. The Commission is able to contribute towards the costs of centres for visistors and information.

The Commission issues a series of specialist publications relating to specific aspects of its work together with the results of its experiments and research. It has accepted a special responsibility for the issue and promotion of the Country Code. Through the medium of this Code those with no knowledge of rural affairs are guided towards an understanding of the elementary principles of how to treat, and how to behave in, the countryside.

Since the origin of the Commission lies in the National Parks and Access to the Countryside Act 1949, its functions in relation to these parks persist. It designates both National Parks and Areas of Outstanding Natural Beauty. As far as National Parks are concerned the Commission discusses and advises on each park authority's plans for the park and other matters, maintaining a close liaison with associations of county and district councils, the National Park authorities and their parent county councils. Indeed the Commission is concerned specifically to advise on the appointment of National Park officers and their duties and on the appointment by Ministers of persons to National Park boards and committees which advise the former on the administration and operation of the National Parks. Parallel with its concern with countryside information services generally runs its specific concern with such services in the National Parks.

Each park is administered by a single committee or board no matter whether the park area lies in one or more counties. This authority is made up of members appointed by the local authorities concerned and by the Secretary of State. The park authorities are responsible for most development control in the parks, and exercise certain conservation and recreation powers; they also undertake such functions in the parks as may be arranged with the county or district councils concerned. The normal planning authorities retain responsibility for the preparation of local and structure plans except where the parks are administered by boards. Where this is the case, the boards have the responsibility for the preparation of these plans. At the moment only the Peak and the Lakes parks have boards.

Areas of Oustanding Natural Beauty are designated by the Commission under Section 87 of the National Parks and Access to the Countryside Act 1949. After designation these areas are specially controlled, as far as the preparation and implementation of development plans are concerned, by the planning authorities across whose boundaries they fall. The primary purpose of a designation is to strengthen the power of the local authorities to protect the landscape of the area through policies in the development plan, through development control and by positive action. Where development plans are prepared for designated areas planning authorities must consult the Commission. In a letter (which was published in the *Seventh Report of the Countryside Commission*)

to county and district councils responsible for Areas of Outstanding
Natural Beauty, the Assistant Director said:

The Commission fully recognise that local authorities carry the prime responsibility
for the conservation of Areas of Outstanding Natural Beauty and that day to day
control will usually be carried out by District Councils. But the Areas themselves
have been designated under Statute for their national importance. The Commission
urge local authorities, therefore, to accord these Areas special attention in formulating and executing policy and to adopt appropriate machinery to ensure consistent
policy throughout the area.

The Commission promotes the establishment of long-distance routes
throughout the countryside and meets the whole of the cost of creating
and maintaining these routes. They are also developing the range of their
work in connection with footpaths generally by grant-aiding work on
special footpaths and bridleways and by improving the standard of
footpaths.

In the field of planning the Commission has a part to play which, as
public concern about the protection of the countryside deepens, is
growing in importance. It gives advice to planning authorities on certain
aspects of their structure plans and is, from time to time, also involved
with local plans. In the even wider sphere of countryside policy the
Commission is consulted by government, usually in the first stages of
policy formation. The Countryside Commission is financed through the
Department of the Environment subject to its submitting an annual
budget. In the event of a dispute between the Department and the Commission the latter has a right of appeal direct to the Treasury. Once the
budget has been approved and the money forthcoming, the Commission
is not subject to undue constraint on the detailed use of its funds.

# CHAPTER FOUR

# The Public Sector

Under Sections 7, 8, 9 and 10 of the Countryside Act 1968 local authorities may provide certain facilities and carry out certain works in country parks, on common land and on camping and picnic sites: for example, they may put up buildings, do site works, make parking places and allow, or provide for, sailing, boating, fishing and bathing. These powers may be exercised on land which the authorities themselves own, or which does not belong to them subject to such terms as may be agreed with the owners. Where necessary they may acquire compulsorily land where it is needed to enable them to carry out their functions under the Act.

This part of the book is primarily concerned with these powers and functions and with the relationships between the county councils and district councils who use them. The Countryside Act provides that in exercising their powers on any land, county councils shall consult the appropriate district councils in which the land lies and obtain the consent of any other county council concerned, and that where district councils propose to exercise their powers they shall obtain the consent of the county councils concerned. Close co-operation, therefore, is necessary between the appropriate councils at different levels: the superior council having the obligation only to consult, the inferior council having the obligation to obtain the superior council's consent.

As a result of these provisions the Countryside Act has been implemented in different ways in different parts of the country. In some cases a county council has taken the initiative and has set up an organization for the establishment and running of countryside recreational facilities and in doing so has taken on the planning and subsequent management function. In other cases a county council has seen itself as having a responsibility to advise district councils on the implementation of the

Act, but, on the whole, not to become involved in detailed initiation nor in subsequent management. In yet other cases an organization between these two extremes is in being under which a county council is both adviser to the districts within its boundaries and also initiator and manager of the larger schemes of countryside recreation. In virtually all cases, however, the organization is mutable and may develop one way or the other as people, politics and finances alter. But since each county is unique in its landscape, its urbanization, its nearness to the sea, the needs of its inhabitants, the degree of invasion which it suffers from across its borders and the opportunities which exist for the provision of public leisure areas, each may equally claim the right to a unique organization. A county may have certain natural features which specifically call for careful and co-ordinated development for leisure. Through Berkshire, for example, run the River Thames and the Ridgeway route across the Downs and the county council has seen its responsibility as being primarily one of giving advice and of co-operating with adjacent and adjoining authorities in planning and controlling the use of these special features. Cheshire, on the other hand, has set up a specialized Countryside and Recreational Division to deal in detail with the particular needs of a large urban population within and just outside its own boundaries; needs which in the estimation of this authority could not be satisfied by leaving the prime responsibility with the district councils.

On the whole it seems that counties beyond the pull of London but with large towns or cities within easy reach of their countryside, have tended to set up separate and more or less autonomous countryside leisure departments and have taken to themselves the main responsibilities for recreation. In some cases, however, such leisure provision, regarded as being primarily a county responsibility, has been tucked in under the wing of existing county departments. These departments are usually the County Planning Department and the County Valuation and Estates Department (the exact names vary): the former having the responsibility of planning and selecting sites for country parks, picnic sites and the like and for their design and layout; the latter for their acquisition, development and subsequent management. Usually the two departments act in concert with each other; one department carries more weight then the other all the time, otherwise the responsibility shifts as planning is succeeded by development and development by management.

Where a separate County Recreation Department is in being, its constitution and responsibility have often been a matter of debate, for there is no clear line between, say, what is recreation and what education.

Consequently argument has centred on the inclusion in such a department of responsibility for indoor and outdoor sport, physical recreation, arts, drama, libraries, archives and museums as well as country parks, picnic sites and footpaths.

A difficulty which is endemic in this field in both the public and private spheres is that of assessing the degree of demand for leisure facilities and of determining what the public want, or need, and the probable degree of use to which anything provided will be put. It is this aspect of policy which must give most concern to many officers charged with the initiation and management of leisure facilities in the countryside, for it is on the assessment of likely demand that site selection and design are normally based. If that assessment is wrong, the result is the provision either of facilities which are underused and therefore relatively expensive to maintain or of facilities which are inadequate to cope with demand. Day to day management of sites, in terms of the proper use of resources, is easy where provision and demand are in balance.

Policy-making is, of course, a function of the council concerned and this is usually exercised through the appropriate committee or sub-committee. Most county councils have either set up Recreation and Leisure Committees or Countryside Committees or existing committees have spawned appropriately named sub-committees to deal with countryside matters. These committees may have a rather narrow recreational brief, or may be charged with recommending action to the council on a whole range of matters such as conservation of the countryside and the coast (where appropriate), recreation and leisure, trees and woodlands, wildlife, services of interpretation and information and co-operation with other relevant bodies such as the Nature Conservancy, the Forestry Commission, the National Trust, and the Regional Water Authority. These committees are serviced and advised by the appropriate officers of the council's departments concerned, such as the planning department, the estates department, the education department and, of course, any special department which may have been set up specifically to deal with countryside recreation and leisure.

Countryside and recreation policy-planning is the first aspect of a single problem, the second aspect is the physical management of the facilities provided on the ground, be they laybys, picnic sites, walks or full-scale country parks containing a number of different attractions. Here a pattern seems to be forming which is common to most authorities though, of course, the detail of the pattern will vary in accordance with the number and scale of the recreational facilities provided. A wardening, scavenging and maintenance service is obviously necessary. In many instances the latter two functions can be carried out by, or with the assistance of, the district councils concerned where they are able and willing to include these functions among the duties of their existing staffs. Sometimes the repair and maintenance of equipment, services, fences, gates, car-park surfaces and the like are undertaken by an itinerant maintenance staff under the control of the appropriate officer of the county council; sometimes each country park of sufficient size may have its own repair staff. Often there is both peripatetic and static staff. Where a council has woodlands under its control, a forestry officer, foresters and woodmen may be permanently employed who will, from time to time (such appears always to be a woodman's duty) undertake odd-jobs related only marginally to the countryside and often little to trees or timber. Wardening, on the other hand, is something which has grown naturally with the provision of country parks and picnic sites. The country-side warden is a person whose professional parentage extends from the park-keeper through the ranger, the gamekeeper, the gillie, the botanist, the entomologist and the ornithologist, and skirting narrowly around the policeman! The warden is a very special person, who ranges from the professional on-site manager/chief warden to the ranger-warden-mainten-ance man who understands the countryside and, importantly, under-stands how to deal with people. People who vary from the knowledgeably inquisitive walker and irritably frustrated caravanner, to the truculent and tiresome teenager or the individual with peculiar habits. A chief warden it is who normally works as on-site manager in the case of an extensive country park (he may today be given a deservedly grander title) or who, lower in the status-scale, is in charge, as overseer, of a number of resident or peripatetic wardens. Wardens, to distinguish them from Chief Wardens, may be called Rangers. At this level of responsibi-lity and of immediate contact with the public, it is common practice to provide the warden with a uniform (or at the very least an armband) which clothes him with a degree of officialdom and of identification which the public is in the main prepared to accept. The style of the uniform is important in that to many people it indicates the function of the wearer, and indeed his likely attitude and knowledge. In country parks near big towns the ranger may have to deal with people whose attitude may be aggressive and whose knowledge of the countryside very limited, and it has been found sometimes helpful to him to be accompanied by a large dog. On the other hand, the patrolling of an area by rangers in dark blue uniforms with alsatians at their heels rather spoils the hoped-for

impression that this is a quiet spot in the countryside available for
enjoyment of the air and peaceful exercise!

Most local authorities are, understandably, careful about making any
admission charges to the countryside facilities which they provide, being
willing to meet the annual running cost out of their normal rate income:
where, however, special services are available which can easily be charged
for, then charges are made. Such charges include those for fishing (by the
sale of day-tickets or by leasing water to a local club) or boating or the
use of caravan or camping sites. It may well be that the number of services
where separate charges are made will increase in the future — partly
because the public gets used to the idea of having to pay, partly because
the authority feels that there must be a limit to the unreimbursed
expenditure which can be met annually out of public funds, and partly
because the number of special attractions provided within the near-town
country park will increase. Currently admission or car-parking charges
are rarely made by local authorities though a number are now considering the economical (and political) possibility of charging for cars with a
view at least to meeting the cost of providing and maintaining the car
parks. In any event many councils take a pragmatic view of imposing
charges in that it is clearly pointless to make a charge unless the costs of
collection (including the overhead costs of management involved) are
markedly less than the gross receipts.

Since the heyday of public expenditure on recreation in the countryside in about 1972 the amount of public provision has dropped considerably, but when finance is again more readily available it is reasonable to
expect that councils and their advisers, being now more knowledgeable
on the subject of recreation, will tend to concentrate their resources on
developing areas already in hand and confining new recreational ventures
to suitable sites on the urban fringe. Such sites may well provide facilities at a higher intensity than that at which facilities are provided in the
more traditional country park and be of themselves smaller in area. They
may be expected to mix sport, recreation and education more closely
and to have buildings which can conveniently be used both in summer
and winter. While interpretation in the countryside may be more
logically carried out by means of nature-trails and guided walks, countryside interpretation through indoor exhibitions on these urban-fringe
sites could be rewardingly successful throughout the year by reason that
the buildings in which the exhibitions are housed could be used for
different purposes at all times and seasons. A further advantage of the
urban-fringe recreational sites is that they may relieve pressures on the

more remote areas which are in danger of being overused and thus spoiled.

As management knowledge and expertise improve most authorities are now producing management plans both for any new areas to be brought into use and for existing areas for which no such plans were originally in existence. The shape of management plans will depend upon the county concerned and its recreational organization. They may be documents which provide the outline and some of the details of the county management organization, of the functions of its constituent parts, of the degree and method of control of expenditure (both capital and revenue) and of such things as interpretation, maintenance, traffic and car-parking control. On the other hand, plans may be produced for the management of each individual country park and for each individual area of the county which is subject to a separate management organization. As mentioned in Chapter 3 the Countryside Commission insists on the production of a management plan before it will consider providing grant aid.

As each county's organization for recreation provision is different it is not possible to describe one which is typical, but investigation has shown that where a county has created a special department with responsibilities for recreation and conservation a fairly consistent management pattern is emerging. It should be noted that such a department nearly always has the two functions of conservation and recreation to deal with, and this would seem consistent since it reflects the main functions of the Countryside Commission under whose advisory eyes the county will be working. Understandably the nomenclature of the officers, the departments and their constituent parts differs. Usually the whole is in charge of a director who has a deputy. Apart from his duties on behalf of the director, the deputy sometimes has certain functions specifically allocated to him as his primary responsibility. The department is divided into a number of sections such as countryside, sport and physical recreation, development, arts and administration, each of which may be in charge of a designated officer. The countryside section itself is usually subdivided into management (or manageable) sectors corresponding with areas of the county (e.g. north, south, central) under a responsible officer who is likely to have a wardening or ranger staff to control within his sector. In addition specific country parks or other identifiable units may be carved out of the sectors and given their own management, technical and wardening staff.

Provision is usually made either within the countryside section or in separate sections for forestry, maintenance, interpretation, footpaths and rights of way. The structure of the other sections such as sport and physical recreation, arts and the like are usually less complex than is that of the countryside and recreation section, for the physical distribution of their facilities is less wide and the range of their functions more easily defined. In addition to the specific sections of the type mentioned above there is usually also an administration section which deals with the finance of the division, with design and development generally and probably with certain staff appointments.

Despite the obvious autonomy which a countryside division of this nature enjoys, it is still a matter for precise discussion and agreement as to where the major responsibility begins. Conflict, if that is indeed the right word, sometimes lies between the new department and the existing planning department, for the former understandably needs to be concerned in the earliest stages of planning for recreation, in both the physical and social spheres (e.g. consideration of the type of facility which should be provided, for whom and where), yet the latter, equally understandably, maintains that it is these questions that planners are trained to answer. In the end the right answer is surely that there is no exact boundary between the functions of the two departments and that in the sphere of planning for recreation each must be involved in concert with the other. A properly staffed countryside recreational and conservation department would however expect to take on the detailed design once, in co-operation with the planners, the need, type, function and situation of a recreational area had been established.

The evolution of the so-called National Parks of England and Wales has had a chequered history from the build up of the development of the conservation and outdoor recreation lobbies, which culminated in their designation and establishment under the National Parks and Access to the Countryside Act 1949. Original intentions that the newly created national parks should be administered by autonomous planning boards were only realized in the Peak District and Lake District. For the remainder this model was diluted as a result of lobbying between central government and the constituent local authorities and delegation of power to the county councils within whose administrative areas the parks fell. Even the Countryside Act 1968 can be seen as diverting national policy away from the National Parks and other parts of the countryside with a consequent lack of national co-ordination in the administration and planning of National Park areas. The one notable exception to this lowering of the National Park ideal has always been the Peak District

National Park — debatably facing the greatest pressures and conflicts yet demonstrating the greatest degree of discretion, resolution and imagination.

During the early 1970s the reorganization of local government was coincident to the work of the National Park Policies Review Committee, established in 1971.

To review how far the national parks have fulfilled the purpose for which they were established, to consider the implications of the changes that have occurred, and may be expected, in social and economic conditions and to make recommendations as regards future policies.

The Committee's report was published in 1974.

Some changes in the administration and finance of the National Parks were in part the subject of local government reorganization under the Local Government Acts of 1972 and 1974. The position now is that each National Park is the responsibility of a single National Park Authority advised by a National Park officer heading an independent staff of wardens and other officers. The two planning boards of the Peak and Lake Districts were retained. The Local Government Act 1974 charged each of the National Park Authorities with the responsibility of preparing a National Park plan for submission to the government by 1 April 1977.

The Secretary of State for the Environment and the Secretary of State for Wales in considering the recommendations of the National Parks Review Committee indicated their reactions in the Government Circular (DOE) 4176, which are summarized below. Special emphasis is to be given to the following:

(1) Nature conservation — including encouraging county councils to establish local nature reserves 'to be exercised by the National Park Authority'.

(2) Reinforcement should, and in some cases will, be given to the powers of National Park Authorities relating to making management agreements and pursuing a more vigorous policy of public acquisition when warranted.

(3) There is full recognition of the need for improved co-ordination of agriculture and other rural land uses. On a more positive note the Secretaries of State accept 'that the scope of the Landscape Areas Special Development Order — which requires the agreement of the planning authority to be obtained to the design and external appearance of agricultural buildings which are within the General Development

Order Limits — should be extended to cover siting as well as design and materials; and that the Order should be applied to the whole of every national park'. They go on to indicate their agreement to the principle that farmers 'should be assisted in meeting the extra costs incurred as a result of meeting the stringent design standards appropriate in the national parks'.

(4) There is agreement in principle to the notion that forestry operations should be brought within planning control. This would include Forestry Commission operations to the same extent that other government departments are subject to development control. However, the view is held that the current forestry dedication scheme is adequate to achieve the same degree of effective control without explicitly extending development control to forestry operations.

(5) No immediate action is proposed in regard to the winning of minerals in National Park areas.

(6) The recreational potential of new reservoirs will henceforth be taken into account in considering the siting of new reservoirs.

(7) On the broader issues of employment and housing, there is the suggestion that there should be 'a comprehensive and co-ordinated policy for dealing with the social and economic problems of particular areas by a variety of means appropriate to the environmental quality of the parks'. There is a more specific suggestion that 'suitable light industry would be welcome'. On the question of housing, the twin aims of conservation of amenity and the provision of housing to meet the needs of those needing to reside permanently in the parks are recognized and the role of housing associations in relation to these aims is one suggestion which is currently being pursued.

(8) Support is given for policies on recreational use of the parks to stem from resource management objectives — 'policies for the recreational use of the national parks should be related to the particular qualities and capacities of different types of area'. This statement would, however, appear to give considerable impetus to the use of interpretation as both an educational and management tool — a view supported by the Secretaries of State. Furthermore, on the strength of this statement the potential of the National Parks as tourist centres is also something to be exploited.

(9) So far as the management of facilities for outdoor recreation within the parks is concerned the Secretaries of State endorse all the recommendations for staffing improvements, numbers employed, training and career structures; yet stipulate that these matters must be encouraged within available resources.

Despite administrative difficulties prior to the 1974 reorganization of the administration of National Parks, the duties on the park authorities could be classified under three broad headings which continue to apply:

(a) planning;
(b) implementation;
(c) control.

Before discussing these matters it should first be noted that the planning function of the Peak Park Planning Board is significantly greater than any other of the National Park Authorities. It is, for example, the only one with a sole responsibility for producing a structure plan (under the Town and Country Planning Act 1972) with more strategic importance than the National Park plans already referred to. From this greater over-all responsibility stems a more extensive and positive approach to the planning and management of the Peak Park — its resources, its inhabitants and the visitors to it—than is yet found in any of the other National Parks.

From a land management viewpoint the usefulness of structure plans lies mainly in being able to identify the sources and nature of the trends underlying more detailed policy formulation. In particular the land manager is better able to foresee those areas of his function most likely to be constrained by development control and also those which may afford opportunities for him to explore the possibilities of a more positive role of which he may otherwise have been unaware. Whether or not the land manager is able to benefit from this broader view of planning policy he must work within, or at least alongside, such planning policies as do relate to his area of operation, and in the case of all National Parks the primary source of this background information will be the National Park plans due to be complete by 1977. Up to now, when considering planning policies for rural areas, the land manager has been faced by a planning system more concerned with the urban than the rural environment. National Park plans are, however, expected to extend beyond the rather urban-dominated view of rural planning sometimes encountered to include all the activities for which the park authority has responsibility — many of which have already been mentioned in passing. Recreation, therefore, takes its place alongside all the other problems and issues relating to any given National Park. Invariably it will have sufficient significance to warrant separate treatment but ultimately it will be considered in concert with other issues.

Recreational land management in the National Parks must occur in a planning environment of unusual detail. The external management framework will be more closely defined in these instances; some may interpret this as implying a more constraining effect on management but this would be a most misleading view to adopt. Much of the data collected to form the basis of the plan will be identical to that which the land manager may find useful for his own plans, for obtaining this data is too often beyond the manager's resources. The obtaining of basic data is undoubtedly one of the most expensive requirements of management planning and there are still managers unprepared to take advantage of the wealth of data which may be gratuitously available to them. 'Recreation' constitutes an essential component of National Park plans and is an obvious source of basic data for recreational land managers operating in these areas. The primary areas to which this data will relate are the patterns of supply of and demands for recreation. The analysis of this data as part of the plan will enable the manager to look forward in establishing long-term strategies for his own site — it may, for example, identify opportunities for future development of which the manager could only have become aware by substantial expenditure on research and development.

National Parks, far from constituting areas over which land management functions in the face of draconian controls, could set new standards in rural planning alongside which management could play an inherently constructive role. However, standards of recreational land management must improve in step with improved planning standards.

# CHAPTER FIVE

# Demand for Recreation

Before contemplating the use of land for recreation either in the strategic terms of resource allocation or the tactical terms of optimum use of the existing pattern of resources, consideration must first be given to the question of the demand for recreation. A general introductory discussion of the demand for outdoor recreation quickly gives way to consideration of the nature of demand, its measurement and, finally, its relationship to use.

The outstanding characteristic of the changing pattern of demand for rural land over the past 50 years or so has been the multiple nature of demand for the tangible and intangible commodities which it provides. In addition, there is growing disparity between the demands placed upon rural land by rural commities, which may be considered directly dependent on the land, and by urban society, only indirectly dependent on it for everything other than countryside recreation. In this latter context, the justification for providing resources for outdoor recreation is largely dependent on the nature and extent of demand, much of it arising from urban areas (Fig. 3).

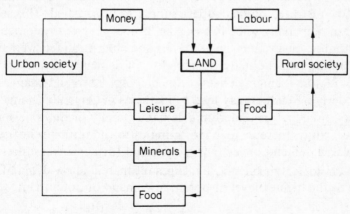

Fig. 3 The relative pressures on rural land

The global nature of the demand for outdoor recreation is of interest to the recreational land manager in that it provides him with a general framework within which more detailed consideration may be fitted, although as the British Tourist Authority/Keele University Pilot National Recreation Survey 1967 states of the pattern of recreation activity, 'only quite local and therefore limited and restricted studies are likely to reveal its full detail'. Despite the implied criticism of local studies, the static (i.e. non-distributive) nature of outdoor recreation means that for most practical purpose the national view must quickly give way to local study. Nevertheless we shall continue temporarily with an overall view of demand for recreation.

Numerous authors have commented on the lack of clarity in the general application of the term 'demand' to phenomena varying from actual or existing behaviour to potential or latent behaviour. An example often cited is that the number of visits to a site is not a measure of 'demand' but of actual behaviour or consumption and may simply be a component of real demand. Much of the confusion arises through the use of different terminologies to describe similar phenomena and is particularly apparent between economics and sociology.

At the first or lowest level of demand, where supply and demand are assumed to be in equilibrium, the economist's definition of consumption (site attendance) equates with the sociologist's definition of actual behaviour. This may, however, be a false situation; actual behaviour will be governed by the availability of facilities. Once these have reached full capacity, an ostensibly stable situation may conceal a frustrated demand. If excess demand exists, increasing the supply of facilities by creating new facilities or increasing the capacity of existing ones allows that demand previously frustrated by inadequate supply to be satisfied. This secondary level of demand may be termed the 'primary increased demand' by the economist, or 'primary need' by the sociologist. So far, we have been assuming that the underlying factors of demand — social and technical factors—remain constant this may not be so and changes in these underlying factors may lead to increases in demand. Changes in the socio-economic factors underlying demand (family incomes, leisure time, etc.) which increase demand, bring us to the third level of secondary increased demand or secondary need and further increases resulting from psychological or technical changes ultimately allow demand to increase to the highest level of potential demand or potential need (Fig. 4)

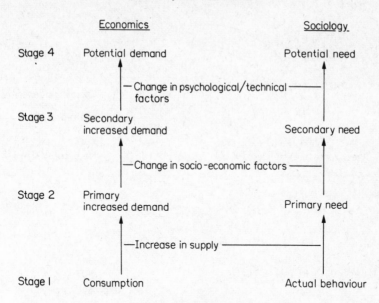

Fig. 4 The stages in realising 'latent' demand

The rigour of the economist's concepts of demand, though valuable for analysis of precise, clearly definable matters, may be less useful in dealing with complex problems which, when dismembered into simple components, lose the inherent complexity around which the problem revolves. Paradoxically, the aggregate demand approach of the economist may be of less relevance to the site manager than the individual-orientated approach of the behavioural scientist. Nevertheless, the rigorous approaches adopted by recreation economists have resulted in clarification of some of the initially nebulous problems surrounding recreation demand. For example, one of the first problems encountered in submitting the consumption of recreational services to economic analysis is the difficulty of defining the commodity consumed and, second, assigning a value to that commodity.

The contribution of Clawson and Knetsch in 1966 was a major advance in this respect. They introduced the concept of the 'recreation experience', a composite commodity comprising:

(a) anticipation and planning of the trip;
(b) the journey to the site;
(c) the on-site stay;

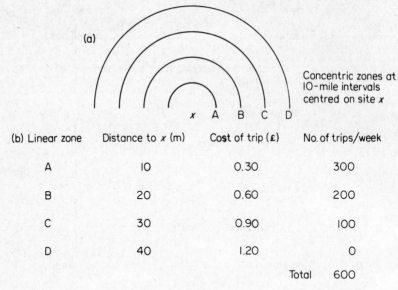

(a)

Concentric zones at
10-mile intervals
centred on site *x*

| (b) Linear zone | Distance to *x* (m) | Cost of trip (£) | No. of trips/week |
|:---:|:---:|:---:|:---:|
| A | 10 | 0.30 | 300 |
| B | 20 | 0.60 | 200 |
| C | 30 | 0.90 | 100 |
| D | 40 | 1.20 | 0 |
| | | Total | 600 |

Fig. 5.

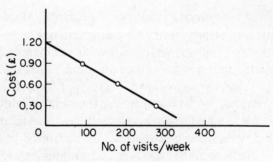

Fig. 6.

| Charge (£) | Total no. visitors |
|:---:|:---:|
| 0 | 600 |
| 0.30 | 300 |
| 0.60 | 100 |
| 0.90 | 0 |

Fig. 7.

(d) the return journey;

(e) recollection of the trip.

This led in turn to estimation of the total benefit of the recreation experience and the price, or cost, of deriving that benefit. Initially, the derived price was expressed in terms of the cost of undertaking the journey. The simplest unit of measurement of the number of recreation experiences per site simply consists of the number of visits per unit of time to the site in question, while the cost of the trip for a non-priced site may be assessed by reference to a costed, distance-decay function. Plotting the cost of the trip against the number of trips per unit period of time, produces a derived demand curve (Figs. 5 and 6).

The analysis may be extended to embrace a situation where a charge is made for use of the site in which case the total cost of the trip is the sum of the travel costs and the entrance-charge to the site. In consequence visitors from zone A now behave as visitors from zone B previously behaved, with corresponding changes in the total number of visitors attending the site as the price varies (Fig. 7). It should be noted that this analysis reflects the effects of changes in price. Numerous studies have been undertaken in Britain and elsewhere to examine this Clawson-type demand curve.

Clawson and Knetsch recognized, however, that demand for recreational facilities constitutes only part of the total demand encompassed by the recreation experience. Consequently site costs must be seen in the context of the overall cost of the trip. Although this and other techniques of demand analysis laying heavy emphasis on the travel behaviour of potential visitors may be capable of some adaptation in attempting to reflect the true cost of travel (involving estimates of the value of time, ease of accessibility to the site, etc.), recreation participation is fundamentally a matter of individual rather than aggregate behaviour. Furthermore, the commodity is not of a uniform, homogeneous nature but determined by the perception of the individual: site attractiveness, the existence of substitute facilities and, above all, quality of management are critical factors which if isolated from the analysis must detract from the overall utility of that analysis to the recreational land manager. Clawson and Knetsch themselves point out that 'if one knew all relationships involved and had reasonably accurate data for the magnitude of each factor in a given situation, one could estimate the volume of recreation that would be demanded, or how many visits a particular site would receive'.

The demand paradox faced by the recreational land manager rests on the problem of aggregating demand. The manager cannot manage for each individual, neither can he manage for every individual: invariably some aggregation of individual visitor preferences is necessary but the degree of aggregation is variable from site to site and manager to manager. Economic analysis takes little account of this variability of aggregation while the manager must determine the degree of aggregation which will be consistent with his management policy.

A land manager cannot reasonably be expected to be thrust into the position of managing or developing recreational facilities with absolutely no knowledge of what he is embarking upon, or at least without being able to acquire some knowledge from other sources. He must have knowledge before he can exercise management judgment. Even the most sophisticated demand analysis leading to the construction of a demand model will ultimately simply constitute an aid to decision-making for the manager. Arguably the manager's own subjective opinion of the pattern of potential demand may offer an equally useful avenue of guidance, if properly analysed. The use of subjective judgment should not be mistaken as an argument in favour of subjective management. The argument is, rather, that oversimplified answers to complex problems may offer the manager little more than he started with; indeed, he may, for a variety of reasons, be persuaded to adopt what is ostensibly 'the' answer without adopting the qualifying assumptions that go with it. In this event he may be better advised to retain the inherent complexity of the problem and an appropriate form of analysis which will accept that complexity, e.g. the application of Bayesian techniques to subjective probability could allow the manager to make his own subjective assessment of a situation on the basis of the information available to him, i.e. retaining the inherent subjectivity of his assessment, but then processing that opinion in a rational and systematic way. Nevertheless, the use of such techniques do not dispense with the need for site-specific data which is an essential prerequisite for management planning.

Recreational land management is centred on the needs of the visitor (or consumer) at a given site. The commodity is created on site and is consumed there. The closeness of the relationship between manager and visitor is apparent. Consequently at an early stage the manager must examine the behaviour of the individual in an attempt to discover what makes him behave as he does.

Three of the basic issues in the psychology of consumption are (1) motivation, (2) perception and (3) learning. Self-fulfilment probably constitutes the most widely postulated derived need motivating individual demand for recreation although there are many other 'drives' which motivate action. Perception — the interpretation of sensations — and learning are both subject areas susceptible to wide-ranging argument as to their relative and total significance. However, it is interesting to note that one of the principal areas of attention in the field of outdoor recreation — that of 'interpretation' — places fundamental reliance on learning, understanding, perception and motivation in encouraging the protection and conservation of valuable resources and, thereby, fulfilling an essential role in relation to resource management.

The social psychologist may equate 'motivation' with the impetus to current behaviour, while 'cognition' determines the nature of that behaviour and 'attitudes' will influence potential behaviour. Of these the one most difficult to quantify yet which probably preoccupies managers most is the latter, 'attitudes' — potential behaviour lying at the focus of management planning.

Inevitably the recreational land manager is managing for groups of participants. Individuals assume a group identity the distinguishing features of which are of primary importance to the manager: frequency of interaction between members; patterns of behaviour distinguishing members of an identifiable group; individual association with groups and identification of a group by external observers. The status of a group or members within it, and the roles played by group members, may be significant to the manager in identifying visitor behaviour and communicating with existing and potential visitors. In this latter respect the manager must also be aware that for directed information to be well received by his intended audience it must be made consistent with the perceived role of the individuals in that audience. Leaving aside for a moment the problem of communicating with potential visitors, communication with on-site visitors is often ineffective, no matter how well intended, because little or no explicit thought is given to identifying the intended audience. Consequently it becomes almost impossible to present the message in a manner appropriate to the audience.

In the research into the demand for outdoor recreation there is a gulf between knowledge of existing and potential patterns of demand, i.e. latent demand. Recreational land management is a relatively recent discipline in a state of flux — who accurately forecast the rise and fall of ten-pin bowling, the popularity of grass skiing or hang-gliding? How far removed these phenomena appear to be from previous patterns of behaviour. But although it is hazardous to identify patterns of latent demand by automatic extrapolation from studies of existing patterns of demand, the manager is investing capital and expertise in attempting to satisfy the demands of tomorrow's visitors as well as today's. Effectively, he has two options: either he accepts a paucity of data and, therefore, the inherent uncertainty of the situation and adopts management techniques appropriate to conditions of uncertainty (these are often mathematically complex); or he clarifies the area of uncertainty to enable himself to employ the rather simpler management techniques appropriate to conditions of relative certainty. It is this latter approach which we shall examine further in attempting to relate latent demand to land use.

Emphasis within the public sphere of countryside recreation has, since the National Park movement, and before, been placed on providing an environment of high natural attractiveness in the belief that this plays a major contributory role in the enjoyment of recreation. This assumption is, however, questionable, it being equally likely that for those enjoying countryside recreation emphasis is placed not on being, *ipso facto*, in the countryside but being actively or passively occupied in the countryside which forms a pleasant and attractive environment in which recreation may be enjoyed often in concert with others and often using equipment of one form or another. The American view in the O.R.R.C. Report 20 (1962) strengthens the hypothesis that a new primary source of enjoyment is not the countryside itself: 'It seems that in many American families leisure time is used not so much for resting and relaxing as to acquire a great variety of skills and interests as well as social contacts.'

The continuing problems of evaluating demand effectively has given rise to criticism of the public sector, in particular, for failing to provide facilities for all sections of the community, criticism arising essentially from non-explicit management objectives in relation to the spectrum of need which exists. As discussed already, at the primary level need tends to be expressed in terms of participation. Provision geared to satisfying this level of need results in stereotyped facilities of the most basic nature often simply a site and access to it. The visitors are left to their own improvisation to derive their own specific enjoyment from the site, in that the facilities do not provide entertainment, simply a pleasant environmen in which visitors must entertain themselves. Such facilities appear, however, to provide recreation for those visitors most prepared to entertain themselves — often the higher socio-economic groups. The example illustrates the potential confusion which arises in investment decisions and

management policy in attempting to reconcile imprecise concepts of
demand with unclear management objectives.

While there may be a tendency for the public sector to allow potential
demand some expression by attempting to satisfy the primary level of
demand: the private sector attempts to solve the same problem by linking
entrepreneurial ability with aggressive marketing techniques then quantifying its management effectiveness in converting latent demand into
effective demand. Of these two approaches the latter presents a more
serious attempt to probe the facets of latent demand. The techniques of
marketing management offer the recreational land manager – in the
public or private sector – greatest immediate potential in exploring this
nebulous area of which the manager must be aware even if he chooses
not to exploit it.

The collection of information about markets and the consumers
comprising them, its subsequent analysis and processing into the most
convenient form for making management decisions is known as 'market
research'. Information may be acquired directly by observation or
surveying and from secondary sources. Consumer observation may be a
fruitful source of information for outdoor recreation, being particularly
useful when researching at a fixed location whether this be a souvenir
shop, country park or National Park. Various recording techniques such
as time-lapse, aerial or infrared photography enable a wide variety of
information to be objectively and systematically recorded. A wide variety
of mechanical monitoring devices are available to assist the manager in
'observing' visitor behaviour, facilitating the subsequent identification of
trends shown up by the collective results. Photographic evidence may
also form the basis for surveying techniques.

Much market information arises from the use of surveys of one form
or other and the choice of survey techniques may have substantial
influence on the effective identification of the potential market available:
its size, the character of actual and potential customers, their geographic
location and their perception of the commodity concerned. Much market
research is applied to strategic aspects of demand on a national or
regional scale. The land manager, concerned with a fixed location and
without the problem of overall allocation of the commodity, may be
able to eliminate certain general market characteristics by predefining
them, e.g. the geographic distribution of potential visitors. The use of
secondary data may be of invaluable significance to the land manager,
particularly where he or she is new to recreational land management or is
attempting to establish a new facility with limited previous experience of

that enterprise.

In certain circumstances the market for a product may be of greater significance than the product itself. It is certainly true in recreational land management that there are numerous examples of modest beginnings being expanded by attention to market requirements rather than simply conserving original resources. Two good examples of this being found at Beaulieu, Hampshire, and Dodington near Chipping Sodbury.

This consumer orientation may be viewed in marked contrast to the production orientation of the traditional enterprises associated with the rural environment — notably agriculture and forestry. In these cases emphasis is placed on maximizing output, particularly by harnessing new technology, and minimizing production costs. The satisfying of customer demand by a greater market orientation to management calls for the subsequent co-ordination of the production or supply processes influencing the visitor.

The overall features of any perfect market are beyond the influence of individual suppliers and although the market for outdoor recreation is by no means perfect the restricted sphere of influence of each facility means that, in general terms, the market is beyond the control of a single operation. As far as the market itself is concerned we start at the fundamental truism that differences do exist between visitors. The initial implication of this will influence the management policy of the recreational land manager in that invariably choices will be made by the manager, explicitly or not, between potential visitors. This process of market identification and selection is known as market segmentation.

At the one extreme of absolute market differentiation it may be said that each individual visitor constitutes a significant market segment by virtue of the uniqueness of his needs. At the other extreme lies the policy of undifferentiated marketing where the peculiarities of individual visitors are ignored, attention being given to their common qualities in an aggregated market approach. Not surprisingly these extreme policies seldom occur. In the former case, the cost of tailoring production and investment to the needs of every individual visitor is prohibitively expensive while ignoring all individualistic factors, considering only the broadest market segment of the market, as in the latter case, may lead to situations of frustrated demand in the smaller segments and hypercompetition in the larger ones. Whether a differentiated or undifferentiated marketing policy is adopted, the necessity for market analysis remains.

In recreation enterprises the manager needs to identify categories of visitors with differing interests, susceptibilities, behaviour, etc.

Certain conditions attaching to market research have been identified by Kotler which, as they become fulfilled, increase the relevance and usefulness of visitor characteristics or behaviour. The three conditions which he specifies are as follows:

(1) *Measurability* − the degree to which information exists or is obtainable on various buyer's characteristics.

(2) *Accessibility* − the degree to which the firm can effectively focus its marketing efforts on chosen market segments.

(3) *Substantiality* − the degree to which segments are large enough to be worth considering for separate cultivation.

The difficulty associated with the first condition boils down to the effective identification of visitor preferences. Price for price and given equal opportunity, would visitors prefer, for example, to purchase an ice-cream or feed the dolphins? The second and third conditions are often associated with identifiable market segments and must be sufficiently substantial to warrant special marketing considerations (to some extent this will be a function of the objectives of management), although it may be possible to identify a market segment which is inaccessible in isolation to others.

One of the justifications put forward for the rudimentary nature of many of the outdoor recreation facilities provided by the public sector and for the hesitancy of private landowners to commit land and capital to recreation provision is the fickle nature (elasticity) of demand bearing in mind the expense of specialized facilities and the unsettling significance of the substitute effect. Whether or not this intuitive argument is justifiable, the manager who has effectively utilized a policy of differentiated market segmentation has the advantages that; first, he is in a position to identify and compare marketing opportunities; second, he can use his knowledge of the marketing response differences of the various market segments to guide the allocation of his total marketing budget; and third, he can make finer adjustments to his enterprise management and marketing appeal.

Research into participation in outdoor recreation has suggested a number of factors which have been shown to have an effect on site attendances and, as mentioned before, these simply correspond to many of the variables commonly used as a natural basis for market segmentation in many spheres of commerce, 'because they have proved to be good predictors of differential buyer response' (Kotler). A non-exhausitive list of segmentation variables, some of which may not have been subject

to research with specific reference to outdoor recreation, are given below
with some comments by Kotler to explain their significance.

(1) *Geographic variables* (e.g. climate, infrastructure, population densi
and distribution): 'most sellers recognise geographic variations within
their market.' Land managers have always contended with these variable
and are probably as adept in considering them as other managers though
their specific relevance to recreational enterprises may be relatively new.

(2) *Demographic variables* (e.g. age, sex, income, occupation, educatic
'have long been the most popular basis for distinguishing significant
groupings in the market place. One reason is that these variables correlat
well with the sales of many products; another reason is that they are
easier to recognise and measure than most other types of variables.' This
suggests that the research in the field of recreation demand is now catch-
ing up to the levels accepted in business management.

(3) *Personality variables* (e.g. gregariousness, conservatism, leadership,
domesticity): 'for some products and brands, personality variables may
lie at the bottom of differences in buyer behaviour... yet the final proof
of the extent of personality segmentation must rest on statistical evidence. Sorely needed is a better set of tests for measuring personality
difference'. Obviously the same problems exist in relation to recreation
although some sites (mainly privately run) do attempt to obtain this
type of visitor data. The noteworthy implication here is that business
managers, aware of the inadequacies in this area, are seeking to improve
their methods of assessment.

(4) *Buyer-behaviour variables* (e.g. usage rate, buyer motive, visitor
loyalty, price sensitivity, quality sensitivity): 'Variables which describe
one aspect or another of the buyer relation to a specific product may
be called buyer-behaviour variables... and can be quite useful in segment
ing a market.' This fairly mild comment conceals what constitutes
possibly the most important category of variables for outdoor recreatior
indeed the inter-relation of several of these factors may be the key to th
optimum utilization of recreation resources in the light of the whole
spectrum of demand to which they are subject.

Having considered the variables likely to have an influence on the
existing or potential market, the manager should be in a position to
determine his marketing strategy. He may decide upon an undifferentiat
marketing policy, concentrating only on the factors common to the
entire market; he may decide to market to all segments, adopting different plans for each (differentiated marketing) or to concentrate his

marketing effort on specific market segments (concentrated marketing). In most recreational land management instances a concentrated marketing strategy is likely to prove the most practicable. Both undifferentiated and differentiated strategies are likely to be hampered by restraints on the availability of resources — unless they are outweighed by other factors such as the unique attractiveness of the site — and by the accessibility of the market which is likely to be constrained by geographic factors, if nothing else.

In any selective marketing approach the manager must evaluate each segment to establish the value of operating in any given one. Each segment should be considered separately, then the potential of each, when aggregated together, will be a prime determinant of the marketing policy. An initial sieving will reduce the number of segmentation variables to those most significant to any given site and at this stage the manager must identify conflicting variables which must either be reconciled or over-ridden. For example, on a site where emphasis is placed on a high-quality 'image' the fact that visitors may prefer to purchase cheap, but inferior souvenirs may be incompatible with the general image.

The marketing policy which is evolved should be worked into the management plan for the whole project and the manager must decide on the degree of market orientation to which the management plan will be subject. In so doing he must also distinguish between matters within that policy which may be implemented within the scope of site management and those which may require separate attention, which for the sake of definition will be referred to as 'marketing' in a specific sense. The selection of market segments will be facilitated by quantitative evaluation of demand stemming from those segments.

When a manager is faced with providing facilities to satisfy a composite demand complicated by cross elasticities of demand, he needs to define his market in a systematic manner which identifies its components without necessarily reducing complexity of their interaction. The discussion so far has rested on relatively quantitative aspects of demand Further analysis is required to yield more quantitative data for market planning: three primary dimensions of demand measurement are suggested. Those dimensions are the nature of the product itself, its potential geographic distribution and the planning time periods (long, medium, short). For recreation the distribution of the market will be of more relevance than the distribution of the commodity. There has been a proliferation of management terms to describe different facets of demand relevant to different management purposes — goals, target, quotes, forecasts, etc.

Most of these terms are applied either to the market for a product or
service or the share of that market available to a particular enterprise.

The recreational land manager may define the demand for the site and
facilities offered for recreation over a given time period as the volume of
consumption that would be achieved by a defined visitor spectrum, in a
known geographical area in a static marketing environment under a defin
marketing programme. Volume of consumption is frequently expressed
as a number of visitors to the site. Such a measure is useful when the site
is relatively homogeneous — i.e. no outstanding features — although preoccupation with visitor numbers may serve to encourage homogeneity
in the provision of facilities. When the site or facilities on it are priced,
financial income or turnover may be appropriate measures of consumptic
Problems of definition in this matter may arise where, for example, a car
carrying a family group of five arrives at a site, three of the group leave
the car and enter the site leaving the remaining two in the car: despite
the fact that all five may benefit from the recreational experience, shoulc
the two persons remaining in the car be counted as visitors? The answer
will depend on the management objectives for the site — if they are
simply geared to provide public enjoyment the answer is likely to be
'Yes', but if they are also seeking to derive financial revenue then the
answer will be 'No'. Similarly management objectives will determine the
matter of defining the visitor spectrum which may embrace all or part
of the total market. The geographic definition of the market area should
be as explicit as possible and for the local market this does not normally
present difficulty. However, the opportunity should not be lost of
identifying as yet unforeseen areas of demand, possibly remote from the
site but from which demand may nevertheless materialize.

Most managers will be operating in an environment defined by a
framework of polictical, legal and financial constraints over which they
have little or no influence. Nevertheless, changes in these factors may
have a far-reaching influence on management planning and therefore,
when forecasting market demands, the manager be aware of the factors
to which he plans will be sensitive and the extent to which changes in
these variations will invalidate his forecasts. This sensitivity will, among
other things, be a function of the time period over which the plan
extends — the larger the term, the greater the likelihood of forecasts
being adversely affected by unforseen influences. The time period over
which demand is to be forecast will determine the certainty which can
be attached to the forecast. Having considered the effect of the external
management environment, the internal environment, i.e. that over

which the manager has complete control, will also influence market demand. For example, variations in price and/or quality are likely to result in changes in demand (depending on the elasticities of demand) and the rate of change will indicate the sensitivity of the market to those changes. The extent to which management plans are orientated towards the behaviour of the market will determine responsiveness to market changes.

The degree to which marketing-orientated management can influence market demand must lie between the limits identified by the level of primary demand (site attendance) which occurs without stimulating demand and total potential demand. The difference between these two limits represents the marketing sensitivity of demand. If the planned or forecast level of demand for a site exceeds primary demand, that forecast will be determined by the market demand equating to a given level of marketing effort. Similarly where there is competing supply for specified market segments, it is likely that the proportion of any segment in question attracted to any given site will be proportional to the marketing effort there (normally measured by reference to the budget allocated to marketing), the effectiveness of that expenditure and the elasticity of the market share with respect to effective marketing effort. In forecasting the planned market share for an enterprise, some estimate must also be made of the magnitude and efficiency of the expenditures of competitors on their own marketing plans. In a stable marketing climate the extrapolation of present trends may form a credible base for estimating future market shares, but stability is seldom present in the marketing of recreation facilities and in more volatile circumstances forecasts must be made from assumptions which are likely to require continual revision. Depending on the site capacity and the level of investment allocated to it, the forecast operating capacity of the site will be dependent on the marketing activity incorporated in the management plans for the site.

Once the potential market has been fully defined, the data may already be available to enable total market potential to be measured but the forecasting of future demand for a particular site is likely to be rather more difficult. The more unstable the demand, the more hazardous forecasting becomes, yet at the same time accuracy becomes increasingly important and forecasting procedures are likely to become more elaborate. The planning process is fully dependent on the information fed into it. Any manager must, therefore understand the problems of forecasting in order to be in a position to evaluate the forecasts upon which he must make his decisions.

The three facets of behaviour which form the basis for forecasting demand are (a) past behaviour — in that this may condition future behaviour; (b) present behaviour — in that this behaviour may continue; and (c) people's opinion of the future behaviour of themselves or others. The numerous techniques which have been developed to forecast demand stem from these three basic elements.

Time series analysis and statistical demand analysis are two examples of forecasting techniques based on the results of past behaviour. The former simply examines past competition as a function of time, it does not seek to determine the underlying causal factors of demand although some, if not all, may emerge from analysis of the patterns of consumption over time and is particularly useful where the factors underlying demand are stable. The technique is based on scrutiny of the time series of past visitor attendance (or consumption) to yield indications of future behaviour, and to be fully exploited there needs to be a systematic variation in consumption over a given time period. Such variations may be described as trends, cyclical, seasonal or random. In relation to demand analysis, trends identify the continuing effect of variations in demand. They are, therefore, normally of a long-term nature often arising as a result of external factors. The isolation of cyclical variations is more likely to be relevant to medium-term forecasting, while seasonal variations may be used to describe any recurrent pattern of consumption and more frequently relate to short-term fluctuations. Any time series is likely to include variations with an apparently random frequency of occurrence and it is part of the analyst's job to determine any systematic patterns in the series.

Orthodox time-series analysis normally involves the reduction of a pattern of consumption in the given time into the four variation categories trends are conventionally expressed in absolute terms and the others in a percentage of the trend variation. Orthodox analysis has been ammended to facilitate rapid yet extensive application of the technique by 'approximation' factors — exponential smoothing' — to yield a forecast which averages past consumption but gives greater weighting to more recent sales levels. In other words, a fairly simple method of updating sales forecasts. Time-series analysis is inadequate when it becomes necessary to discover a direct relationship between patterns of consumption and patterns of demand. Statistical demand analysis provides a means of uncovering these relationships in attempting to analyse the significance of the factors that affect the demand for a site. Indeed, even when it is inadequate as a forecasting technique, the knowledge of these factors

which this analysis is likely to generate will be useful to the manager. One
aspect of statistical demand analysis is that it does not necessarily seek
to analyse every factor influencing demand but the 'main' factors.

Given the existence or availability of appropriate data, an equation is
constructed which best fits the data. The derivation of this equation
(sometimes referred to as a demand model) can be greatly facilitated by
the use of computers and this has been intrumental in increasing the use
of this type of forecasting. There is, however, a continued danger that if
a model has been successfully applied in the past its continued use may
replace independent judgment, a problem inherent in this forecasting
technique is the relevance of the demand equation to future demand as
more data becomes available. Apart from the adequacy of data in respect
of the number of variables under consideration, there are several other
problems of which the manager should be aware. The first, multicolinearity,
occurs when some independent variations are not independent of one
other and their effects are difficult to isolate. In such cases it may prove
necessary to drop one of the colinear variables or to attempt to express
them in terms which may reduce the effective colinearity, e.g. expressing them in relative units (e.g. a measure of relative difference). An
uneven distribution of forecasting errors (residuals) resulting from
application of the demand model gives rise to a shortcoming known as
'autocorrelation of variables'. Although it may be impossible to overcome any residual errors, they should only arise as a result of the influence of random variables, consequently any constant maldistribution
would suggest that some systematic variable remains unidentified. Finally,
it may be found that there is no single demand equation which satis-
factorily reflects the actual pattern of demand. For example, the effects
of pricing and advertising may have independent influences on demand.
This is referred to as 'two-way causation' and requires re-examination
of the demand equation and possibly to formulation of additional
equations to construct a satisfactory demand model.

Passing mention has been made to the study of visitor behaviour. In
the present context this may also form part of a forecasting technique
where this behaviour can be analysed with a view to determining
systematic patterns. Generally the object of such research is to determine
visitors' actual responses to situations of choice which may vary, in fact,
from say the selection of routes within a site to the selection of products
in the souvenir shop. Observation may be continuous and exhaustive
(in analysis of every possible choice at all times) through the probable

resource requirements, for such a blanket approach normally militates in favour of a more selective approach. As often as not the objective of the survey will resolve this question: for a single retail good such as a particular product in the shop the market may be tested by providing the 'choice' and monitoring consumer reaction to it. Where it is necessary to monitor responses to a complete choice spectrum, such as routes within a site, selectiveness may be achieved by restricting the time or area of study. 'Market testing' of this nature may be useful in evaluating short-term visitor reaction.

Possibly the most obvious forecasting technique, yet probably the most difficult to apply successfully, is that of asking people what they believe they (or others) will do. There are three primary sources for opinion surveys: first, visitors, themselves; second, management staff in contact with the visitors; and third, expert opinion. There are numerous practical limitations to forecasting from these sources and always the over-riding problem of assessing the value of largely subjective data in relation to its cost of collection. The cost will of course be dependent on the extent of the survey — particularly size of survey — and the method of interview.

Self-expression on the part of visitors of their opinions and intentions is limited in so far as there may be an inability or lack or willingness to define and communicate information, and the utlimate question must be: will visitors actually behave as they prophesy? Surveying the opinion of those actually dealing with visitors has the intuitive attraction that staff are likely to be both knowledgeable and co-operative. However, for a variety of reasons their opinions are invariably subject to bias which may be difficult to identify or counteract in a small sample of the size which might be expected at most recreational sites. Where expert opinion is readily available, it may provide an attractive variation on the staff survey. It can be quickly and cheaply surveyed and is likely to be capable of producing balanced views. Nevertheless, the analyst is faced with opinion, not fact, and the problem of identifying good and bad opinion becomes even more critical with what is likely to be a reduced sample size. A further consideration is that opinion is most credible when used to produce a composite view and cannot easily be analysed to derive dissected views. Consequently the use of opinion surveys is more appropriate for aggregated, rather than breakdown, forecasting.

Numerous problems beset attempts to forecast demand and the manager must be continually aware of when to adjust his forecasting methods to respond to (or ignore) these problems. New demand factors may arise at any time for any site. Dependent and independent variables may be equally difficult to forecast. The demand equation may lack subtlety in the manner in which variables are incorporated in it; for example, a model incorporating a simple income variable may conceal the fact that total income may be less relevant than its distribution. The selection of particular forecasting techniques will be influenced by a variety of internal and external considerations such as availability and reliability of data or the stability of demand. As the questions of future demand to which forecast answers are sought become increasingly complex, their solution may require a combination of techniques. The results of forecasting can invariably be improved, notably by improving the quality of the data analysed and by improving (or introducing improved) forecasting techniques. Such improvements generally have to be bought and the effectiveness of this expenditure should therefore, be evaluated beforehand. The inadequacies of present methods must be examined with regard, for example, to the extent of present levels of error, their management significance and the sensitivity of present forecasts to variations in the underlying assumptions on which they are based.

A simplified example may help to outline the main considerations in preparing a marketing plan as part of an overall management plan.

Nonesuch Park in the central midlands includes a Georgian mansion overlooking a lake set in 40 acres of landscaped parkland. A fighter aircraft of First World War vintage is stored in an old barn and is capable of restoration. A number of wartime curios have been assembled in the house over the years. It was decided to exploit the recreational potential of the park, the house and grounds were opened during the spring and summer of last year as an initial experiment to test the market. After an encouraging response a more accurate assessment of potential usage is now sought.

Some primary data is available from the following sources:

(1) A visitor survey was undertaken by a group of students.
(2) On the summer bank-holiday (which marked the highest daily attendance) a set aerial photographs of the site were taken.
(3) Informal discussion with visitors.

Secondary data for an evaluation procedure is available from a variety of sources:

Stage 1 – define local conceivable market.
Stage 2 – consider market strategy.

Stage 3 – define market segments by application of segmentation variables.
Stage 4 – determine marketing policy.
Stage 5 – prepare marketing plans.
Stage 6 – promoting the plan and implementing the marketing programme.

*Stage 1*
Definition of the total market: This is not the place for weak hearts and so to avoid underestimation the population of the country is taken here.

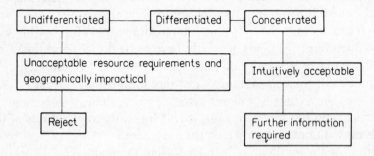

Fig. 8 Marketing strategies

*Stage 2*
Market strategy is shown in Fig. 8: Initially, undifferentiated approaches may be adopted in order to stimulate primary demand by making the maximum number of people aware of the existence of the facilities. If this approach may be said to have been adopted for the first season, the present requirement is to review this strategy. Limited financial resources and lack of homogeneity of both the commodity and the market militate towards a selective approach. Some form of concentrated strategy appears most practicable.

*Stage 3*
Definition of market segments: At this stage the potential market is reduced into segments by the application of segmentation variables.
    (1) *Geographic variables*:
        (a) The local and regional road network facilitated north–south traffic movement, but east–west circulation is less easy. (The M1, 5 miles away, presents a considerable barrier.)
        (b) Site access is good but unsignposted.
        (c) Transport services are poor – the nearest rail and bus links are

respectively 12 and 4 miles away. (The visitor survey indicated that 95 per cent of visitors travelled by private vehicle or walked and this is borne out by observation.)

(d) Location − primary and secondary data indicates that the maximum expected journey time for day-visitors to be 45 minutes. (One commercial site in the region works on a 1 hr 15 min maximum time.) On-site data indicates a significant number of visitors calling in to break a longer journey, particularly for north−south routes.

The application of appropriate forecasting techniques, notably statistical demand analysis would facilitate the preparation of a map defining the extent of the present and foreseeable market for day-visitors which might appear as in Fig. 9.

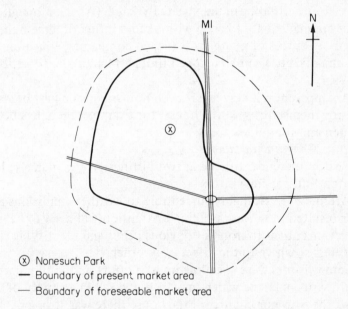

Ⓧ Nonesuch Park
— Boundary of present market area
— Boundary of foreseeable market area

Fig. 9 General location of Nonesuch Park

Although it is unlikely that the wider market for passing visitors can be identically mapped, an alternative mapping notation may be useful, e.g. using a base map of, say, the British individual visitor origins may be identified by pins giving an idea of their distribution.

(2) *Demographic variables*:
After the first season the outstandingly significant factor relating to the visitors themselves was that almost all visitors reached the site on foot or by car. Car-ownership would appear to imply certain levels of income

and occupational status of groups attending the site. It was also found that the groups in the cars were family groups with, therefore, a relatively high overall percentage of children. Apparently at surrounding sites a variety of socio-economic factors have been found to have a bearing on site attendance. The distribution of actual and potential visitors conforming to the car-ownership requirement may be mapped on the market base map. (It may also be worth while identifying similar areas outside the likely market area, if by advertising and promotion they could be attracted to the site.)

(3) *Personality variables*:

(a) It had been intuitively envisaged that the site would attract individual family groups, yet the interest expressed by, for example, local coach firms, has been unexpectedly large. (At the moment the facilities are inadequate to cope with a rapid influx of large numbers of visitors.) Sources of group visits (coach companies, educational establishments, etc.) can be mapped though further identification may be necessary.

(b) An apparent reluctance has been noticed on the part of visitors to seek for themselves — in the house, for example, there has been a strong demand for guided tours.

(4) *Visitor behaviour variables*:

(a) Visitors were identifiable in two distinct groups, namely, local day-visitors and passing visitors.

(b) Attendance was highly susceptible to weather conditions and at times resulted in serious 'peaking'. Attention will need to be given to market incentives to iron out obvious peaks and identifying suitable facilities less sensitive to the effect of weather.

(c) Some visitors were spending up to 5 hours on the site, particularly on return visits, a factor which may be exploited in a variety of ways.

(d) At the souvenir counter in the house there was strong demand for low-quality (and relatively low-price despite high mark-up) merchandise. In general the interaction of price sensitivity and quality sensitivity is unclear but for a variety of reasons (e.g. development control) emphasis will be placed on maintenance of quality as a management objective.

*Stage 4*

Determination of marketing policy: Geographical factors indicate some form of concentrated marketing policy. The segments from which greatest benefit may be expected from concentrated marketing have already been discussed in stage 3. Now, however, the cost of marketing to each segment must be evaluated in relation to the likely benefits to be derived. As concentration increases so marketing policy must become more integrated with overall management. There are two matters which must, in particular, be determined at this stage. These are, first, the time periods to which marketing will be expected to operate and, second, overlap of competition in intended market segments then, having identified levels and sources of competition, the extent to which competition should be active or aggressive.

## Stage 5

Preparation of marketing plans: First, the market factors to which management effectiveness is likely to be susceptible must be identified. At the same time the degree of error likely in their estimation must be assessed. The obtaining of pertinent data must be incorporated in the plan, consequently areas of information requiring quantitative data (e.g. for market forecasting or monitoring management efficiency) must also be identified. The plan must be capable of identifying past behaviour (incorporating comparable evidence) and seeking opinion on future behaviour to forecast future levels of demand. It must also be capable of incorporating onsite information on visitor behaviour, suitably analysed, into the plan and be flexible enough to enable this information to result in continous reappraisal of the plan. Above all, at the planning stage, the marketing objectives are coupled with the resource management objectives which will be considered later.

## Stage 6

Implementation and promotion: In any market-orientated management research is simply one of the starting-points in the management process. Numerous decisions must consequently be made as part of that process but these decisions are less central to the specific matter of demand forecasting which is the subject of this chapter.

# CHAPTER SIX

# *Site Evaluation*

The value of the land resources available to the recreational land manager
will be dependent upon the types and intensities of use to which they can
be subjected. 'Use' represents the interface of supply and demand, though
general terms such as 'recreation demand' or 'recreation carrying capacity'
are too unspecific at the enterprise level. The interface is not uniform
and often land-use decisions will be arrived at by laying greater emphasis
on supply or demand, i.e. resource-determined or activity-determined
uses. Satisfying any demand for outdoor recreation presupposes the
availability of a suitable site; conversely, supply-determined land-use
decisions are investigated on the assumption that either demand already
exists, or is reasonably capable of being generated — stately homes are a
typical example of sites with the resources which offer a focus for immediate recreational use.

Site evaluation in the present context refers primarily to those natural
resources associated with any site having recreation as one of its potential
uses; examples include: land, water, landscape quality, buildings. Land
appraisal is traditionally a financial exercise based on the presumption
that land has value because it can earn rent in some form or other, and
that land will move to its most profitable permitted use. It is clear, therefore, that site evaluation must be related to predetermined or foreseeable uses. It should also be systematic, imaginative and yet as objective
as possible.

Only in the case of rural land does the physical identity of the land
assume anything more than superficial significance in the evaluation
procedure. In urban-type development if we think of the most profitable
permitted use to which a site may be put, the greater the reliance placed
on consumer attraction — namely site attendance (as in the case of
retail or entertainment facilities) — generally, the greater the importance

of consumer accessibility. In other words, the number of substitute locations is inversely proportional to the degree to which consumer accessibility becomes critical. However, in some circumstances consumer
accessibility may be counterbalanced by accessibility to factor inputs
(raw materials, etc.). The same is true, largely, for sites for recreation
facilities, though in the case of countryside recreation where sites, by
definition almost, are relatively remote from urban centres, reduced
accessibility may be counterbalanced by site attractiveness. At this point,
however, the individual, unique properties of the site become increasingly
important, and with this implicit reduction in the homogeneity of the
sites being evaluated, the process of evaluation may become contentiously
subjective.

For many land uses it may be possible to synthesize an 'identikit'
specification incorporating all the relevant factors for the site which
conforms most closely to an 'ideal'. Against such fairly objective yardsticks potential sites may be compared, but in these cases the site 'use'
can generally be expressed simply and explicitly and market conditions
accurately assessed. Where clearly predetermined notions of use and site
requirements exist for outdoor recreation, the same type of processes
may be applied. Such instances lead on to the problems of site selection
and procurement but, although the selection and appraisal of primary
sites may be central to recreation planning, for the land manager this is
a specialist province of little immediate relevance to those already possess-
ing a site which, ideal or not, requires managing. In these cases the primary feature of the site concerned is its fixed location. The combined
significance of location and accessibility is fundamental to any site
evaluation.

The location of the site in relation to the people who it is envisaged
will use it is obviously central to the preparation of any management
plan. A 30-mile radius has proved to be a significant and often adopted
measure of the distance that day-visitors will travel by car at weekends.
But this type of general yardstick can be misleading if, for example,
the location and attraction of substitute facilities is not taken into
account to modify this rule-of-thumb (see, for example, Fig. 10) and
other experience in Britain indicates greater variation in the maximum
range of influence of sites. Moreover, actual physical location may be no
more significant than the perceived location of the site to potential
visitors in the catchment area. Indeed, cognitive distances may be more
significant in relation to visitor attendance than actual distance. There
is much work still to be done on the concept of 'cognitive' or 'mental'

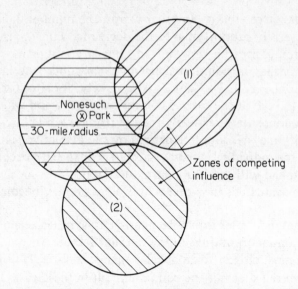

Fig. 10 Overlapping influence of competing sites

mapping relating location and socio-economic factors to obtain some insight into the processes of spatial behaviour.

Attempts have been made to measure site accessibility for recreation projects in objective terms. For example, by assessing the proximity and standard of roads in the vicinity of the site (see M. Blacksell, *Recreation v. Land Use: A Study in the Dartmoor National Park*, Exeter Essays in Geography, 1971) or the number of roads and road junctions in the vicinity of the site (see B. Cracknell, 'Accessibility to the Countryside as a Factor in Planning for Leisure', *Regional Studies,* Vol. I, 1967). Although the manager is likely to have an intuitive working knowledge of the accessibility to sites under his control, the importance of this factor does warrant more than subjective awareness. Furthermore, external accessibility up to the site will often be directly linked to the internal accessibility determined by the infrastructure of the site itself and should, therefore, be considered as an integral part of the visitor flow network.

Though accessibility and location make an essential contribution to the unique nature of any piece of land, rural land has a more complex internal identity composed of all the factors influencing its productive or aesthetic potential. The manager's perception of how these components interact with one other and his awareness of the possible combinations available to exploit will influence his own assessment of the potential value of the land at his disposal for recreational use. For most types of rural land use, knowledge and experience exists to enable those factors influencing the suitability of land for that use to be identified and, possibly, the relative significance of those factors to be measured; soil fertility, for example, constitutes a major consideration in evaluating land to be used for farming. Although as a planning strategy it may be important to conserve areas of high fertility for agricultural use, in a land management context prospective owners may compete financially to own such land. But more pragmatically, the farmer is more likely to be preoccupied with the problem of making the best of the land actually available to him even through this may not be of the highest fertility; he may, indeed, be able to offset the effects of lower fertility by, for example, above-average management.

Ther are numerous factors recognized and accepted as having a significant potential influence on the suitability of land for recreation. Without even attempting to impute a value to that land for that use, knowledge of these factors must be applied in an analytical and systematic manner to evaluate the potential of specific sites for recreation. Potential surface analysis is one established example of such an approach, the aim of the technique being to use surface potential as a yardstick against which independently derived strategies could be measured. First developed in the Nottinghamshire—Derbyshire Sub-regional Planning Study, it was later applied to studies of informal recreation in Sherwood Forest and South Wales. However, identification of use-potential is not necessarily enough to stimulate the exploitation of that potential without further quantification. Like the farmer, the recreational land manager may not be concerned with the management of a prime site but the management of any given site good, bad or indifferent. The process of resource evaluation which he must undertake falls into two parts:

(1) Identification — of factors likely to have any significant potential for recreational use.

(2) Assessment of value — of all the relevant factors individually and in combination.

Unfortunately, the recreational land manager cannot benefit to anything like the same extent as the farmer from centuries of accumulated knowledge of the identification and evaluation of resource potential. If he has a particular recreational use in mind, his task is easier in that he should be able to stipulate, fairly readily, any natural resource requirements.

Otherwise his main preoccupation should be to ensure the optimum exploitation of all the resources at his disposal and in this his initial appraisal must be exhaustive in identification, objective in evaluation and systematic throughout.

The extent or capacity of land to meet the demand for agricultural produce is initially determined by the inherent productive capacity of that land for growing those commodities best suited to the prevailing natural conditions. But referring to the 'capacity' of rural land to supply recreational goods and services is a fundamentally different concept and, therefore, requires some discussion. There are numerous definitions of 'recreational carrying capacity' most of which are biased toward the academic discipline underlying the various authors' interests in recreation. However, a frequently adopted working definition is that found in the Countryside Recreation Research Advisory Group publication, *Countryside Recreation Glossary*, 'the level of recreation use an area can sustain without an unacceptable degree of deterioration of the character and quality of the resource or of the recreation experience'. Thereafter four different types are identified as: (a) physical capacity; (b) ecological capacity; (c) economic capacity; and (d) perceptual capacity. Subdividing the general definition in this way, encourages an appreciation of the many different facets of capacity which collectively or individually may determine the factors which limit further exploitation of available resources. Subsequent definitions have tended to follow this taxonomy, although the four together, in some respects, constitute an unnatural grouping; physical and ecological capacities relate to the site and the natural resources on it (i.e. with a supply orientation). They are concerned with changing conditions over time and tend, therefore, to be useful in relation to resource-orientated planning. Economic and perceptual capacities, particularly the latter, tend to be determined by visitor behaviour and are correspondingly demand-orientated.

Annual physical capacity (A.P.C.) may be defined as 'the maximum number of user use periods per unit area which can be accommodated on a site during a typical year without causing irreversible physical damage to the site, users or equipment'. However, the usefulness of this definition is limited to providing a management yardstick for normative planning; in this context average daily carrying capacity may be simply derived by dividing the annual figure by the number of days in the season. The notion of sustained physical capacity (S.P.C.) per unit area may be more useful to the site manager and this may be taken as the maximum number of user units which can be accommodated on a site at a point in time, suitable for the use without causing risk of exceeding the annual physical carrying capacity assuming normal patterns of usage:

S.P.C. x user periods for which participation possible = potential A.P.C.

This definition introduces the need to determine a point of irreversible physical damage. Although that point may be capable of being defined in fairly absolute terms, it is likely to be largely academic. Most managers will be seeking an intermediate point representing an acceptable level of change to natural resources.

Although this may imply a value-judgment on the part of the manager, a more objective view may be developed by resorting to ecological carrying capacity defined in the *Countryside Recreation Glossary* as 'the maximum level of recreation use, in terms of numbers and activities, that can be accommodated before a decline in ecological value, assessed from the ecological viewpoint'. But here again this definition has been criticized for failing to take sufficient account of any acceptable degree of ecological change away from the desired ecosystem. It appears that, in general, definitions of ecological capacity tend to rely on an acceptance of three conditions, namely that:

(1) There is a most desirable state.

(2) There is a degree of change away from this which is only just acceptable.

(3) Both of these are matters of judgment.

The determination of the ecological changes resulting from differing intensities and frequencies of a recreation activity on the ecosystem does at least provide the manager with an opportunity to bring greater objectivity to the decision as to what ecological change may be acceptable to him for a particular site. In view of the probable variability of this assessment on the part of the manager, he will effectively have four probable attitudes to adopt:

(1) Ensure that recreational activities exert a minimal modifying influence on the ecosystem.

(2) Attempt to retain the essential charactersitics of an ecosystem but otherwise accept changes resulting from recreational use.

(3) Replace those elements of an ecosystem which are more susceptible to pressure from recreational use by components more resilient to recreational activities, implicitly favouring the recreational use where this conflicts with sensitive ecological elements.

(4) Ignore ecological changes resulting from recreational pressure. It almost goes without saying that these policy options will vary from site to site and manager to manager; they will be strongly influenced by the planned period over which the decision will operate and may even vary within sites which can be zoned in relation to recreational and ecological requirements.

Having considered briefly the limitations on recreational carrying capacity which are primarily functions of the natural properties of the site, two other facets of capacity remain — perceptual and economic capacity — whose determinants extend beyond the site itself. The United States of America Conservation Foundation sees perceptual capacity as 'the most subtle and difficult, but in many ways the most important component of carrying capacity'. In the light of such statements it is ironic that definitions of perceptual capacity are so often vague. However the *Countryside Recreation Glossary* provides a starting definition: 'the maximum level of use, in terms of numbers and activities, above which there is a decline in the recreation experience from the point of view of the recreation participant', and goes on to point out that 'different users may have a different view of the perceptual capacity of the same area according to their activity'.

If a potential visitor observes that a site is too crowded for his liking, he will proceed to one where his expectations are fulfilled. Accordingly, overuse of a site could be prevented by the user's reluctance to swell the number of visitors but this is totally inadequate expectation for rational management. First, this type of self-regulating system assumes not only an excess of supply over demand, but also availability of alternative substitute facilities. Second, if visitor density is permitted to increase unchecked, the site will eventually attract crowd-tolerant users whose attitudes and behaviour may differ from visitors comprising the market segment for which the facilities were originally planned. While the manager should be fully aware of visitor attitudes to all factors influencing visitor perception, there is a danger that intuitive assessments on his part are likely to be erratic and misleading. If personal judgment is the only basis on which this appraisal can be achieved, efforts must be made to adopt systematic and objective methods of assessment to the monitoring of visitor attitudes and preferences.

The optimal economic capacity of a recreation facility is more difficult to define than that for many other productive processes. The *Countryside Recreation Glossary* defines economic capacity purely in terms of multiple land use. Considering recreation alone, the benefits

derived by the consumer are themselves dependent on the capacity of the
site or facilities: in other words, the characteristics of the commodity
vary with the level of output. It may be possible to utilize transformation
functions to describe the possible substitutions of one product for another
and so to derive an optimum mix of facilities given a limited spectrum of
alternatives from which to select. In single land-use terms little more can
be defined as economic capacity than that it represents a limiting constraint
to recreation development where economic criteria are followed in developing and managing the facilities – i.e. where marginal costs are equated
with marginal benefits and reallocation of productive resources would not
advance any user group on to a higher level of indifference without a
greater loss elsewhere.

Many definitions of recreation carrying capacity are tailor-made to
suit specific requirements and tend to be an amalgam of the main elements
already described. For some management purposes physical and ecological
capacity may be synonymous, indeed 'environmental capacity' – sometimes referred to in planning studies – which is exceeds where further
use of the site would result in a loss of amenity, incorporates physical,
ecological and perceptual elements of capacity. Awareness of the consti-
tuents of recreational carrying capacity is simply the manager's first step
in assessing the planned capacity of the site.

The matter of planned site capacity will be returned to later, meanwhile we continue with the question of evaluating the natural resources
of the site. For a given site whose natural resource components may be
considered fixed in supply, objective quantification and evaluation of
those resources may be more difficult than measuring the availability and
extent of labour and capital necessary to exploit their full potential.
However, unsystematic or subjective approaches to the problem of evaluation may lead to land-use decisions for which the full spectrum of
alternative strategies has not been investigated. A simple example of one
basis for classifying recreational site potential is found in O.R.R.R.C
(*Recreation for America,* 1962) with the following components:

(a) high density recreation areas;
(b) general outdoor recreation areas;
(c) natural environment areas;
(d) unique natural areas;
(e) primitive areas;
(f) historic and cultural sites.

Although the classification may be crude, it does at least start to introduce

a systematic element: here, for example, resources are classified in accordance with their physical suitability for a range of recreational uses (of a
type often refered to as resource-based activities). It is assumed that the
natural characteristics of the resource environment will be sought by
visitors and, therefore, these use policies are imputed to natural zones.
For land management purposes this type of classification is too simplistic
to be useful. Further information on location, accessibility and market
appraisal must be incorporated before a realistic use classification can be
derived. Recreational land use is, after all, a function of resource and
user characteristics being incorporated together. One of the first attempts
to consider these together was that of Clawson and Knetsch (*Economics
of Outdoor Recreation,* 1969) which has formed the basis for much of
the current thinking on the planning and management of resources for
outdoor recreation.

A first step which a site manager may take in embarking on the
evaluation of resource potential is the preparation of a resource inventory
which should identify not only surface features, but also any underlying
feature having a significant influence on surface use. In its most simple
form this need amount to little more than a list of resource components.
On more difficult sites this 'list' may become unwieldy and lose meaning.
It may, therefore, be advantageous to carry out some preliminary zoning
of the site and classify resources in relation to those zones.

The primary objective of the evaluation procedure is to identify and
rank the differing potentials of the land surface at the manager's disposal
for recreational use. And although the concept of surface potential differs
from the productive potential normally associated with rural land the
practice of appraising agricultural land is relevant to the recreational
land manager, particularly in relation to the use of natural zoning to
bring order to the resource inventory. Farming has evolved its own natural
zones — fields — and agricultural land is invariably assessed not as a whole,
but on a field-to-field basis. The recreational land manager must seek some
similar means of dividing the site into identifiable components. As yet a
conventional means of subdivision has not been evolved and so the
process will vary from site to site but may, for example, be based on
natural feature — lakes, mountains, etc. — or by reference to existing
patterns of use as, for example, in the O.R.R.R.C. classification already
mentioned. Once a method of zoning has been settled on and applied
the land manager, who may be interested in the recreational potential of
his land either as an alternative to or in addition to other possible uses,
will be in a position to identify areas of land-use conflict — where, for

example, agriculture and recreation may clash (or, indeed, where they may be mutually complementary). Even at this preliminary level the land manager has information which may systematically clarify certain strategic land-use decisions paving the way for policy and plan formulation.

Ultimately site appraisal must proceed to the question of identifying and evaluating the natural resources of the site. Identification will in many instances pose few problems:— Fig. 11 though by no means definitive lists some factors which may typically contribute to a resource-based site evaluation and may form the basis of a checklist providing the primary components of most resource inventories. In different circumstances identification may be a major obstacle, particularly as the resources involved become increasingly unique. One such difficulty may be created by sheer scale — Mount Snowdon though unique in its way is no more so than a rare alpine orchid hidden on its slopes. Another problem may be caused by the variability of dimensions involved in quantifying the resource itself. Here, however, there are devices available to assist the manager in this problem: once the manager can designate the dimensions which most effectively describe the resource in question, there are 'scanning' machines capable of extracting from one form of date (e.g. maps or photographs) and expressing it in a different form (e.g. length of hedgerow per unit area of the site, area of water, etc.).

Undoubtedly quantification of unique resources or a wide variety of resources is exacerbated by the lack of comparable units of measurement. There is a tendency, therefore, to resort to purely descriptive analysis to build a 'picture' of overall resource potential. This may be systematic but it is inherently subjective. Without going to the level of sophistication previously mentioned it is possible to restore some objectivity to the more pragmatic approach by presenting the descriptive analysis in tabular form and incorporating in the table or matrix a scoring system for each resource component identified. Figure 11 illustrates very simply how such a scoring or weighting system could be started. Subjectivity may remain but at least the manager is attempting to impose some order on it. The weighting factor or factors will be determined by the particular perspective which the manager adopts towards the resources at his disposal. His perspective will, of course, be coloured by the management objective under which he operates: environmental capacity may, for example, be the over-riding constraint on the potential use to which the resources may be put, the weighting would then be very heavily biased in favour of environmental considerations. It is equally likely, however, that the manager will be more flexible in his attitude to the capacity

| Weighting factor*<br>Site factors | 3 | 2 | 1 | 0 | −1 | −2 | −3 |
|---|---|---|---|---|---|---|---|
| Area | | | | | | | |
| Topography | | | | | | | |
| Aspect | | | | | | | |
| Climate | | | | | | | |
| Geology | | | | | | | |
| Vegetation | | | | | | | |
| Landscape quality | | | | | | | |
| Area of open water | | | | | | | |
| Water courses | | | | | | | |
| Physical features<br>(e.g. caves) | | | | | | | |
| Location | | | | | | | |
| Accessibility | | | | | | | |

\* Internal weighting factor.

Fig. 11 Evaluation matrix

constraints to be imposed on potential use. He may then prefer to apply
a different weighting procedure for each of the four facets of recreational
carrying capacity. These can then be superimposed on one another to
identify particularly sensitive (or particularly insensitive) features so that
the manager can formulate development policies in a more selective
manner. Ultimately, analysis of the natural resources contained by the
site should be designed to reveal any attributes of the site contributing
to its recreational potential.

This sphere of resource evaluation is debatably the area of greatest
technical difficulty for the recreational land manager. It is also the area
probably best served by external expertise in the many specialist facets
of resource evaluation, expertise ranging from that of the ecologist to
that of the landscape architect. The land manager should consider
carefully the benefit he may be able to derive by taking advantage of
the advice of such experts. At the same time he is bound to reflect that
he may have to buy this information or advice and, being a prudent
manager, will assess the benefit of the assistance obtained in the light
of the cost of obtaining it.

The manager may be able to inject greater objectivity into his own resource evaluation by making use (with an appropriate degree of circumspection) of independent yardsticks. An example of this is the M.A.F.F.'s *Agricultural Land Classification* which assesses the agricultural productivity of land, taking into account various physical factors likely to influence productivity – in some instances the factors which bring out the crops also bring out the visitors, though such analogies are by no means watertight!

At this point it is necessary to re-emphasize that ultimately the value of available resources for recreation will be dependent on the use to which they can be put, and the process resource evaluation comes up against demands expressed in terms of activities and pursuits that those resources can or should withstand. Most activities already appear in various classifications which themselves constitute useful aids in the systematic consideration of activity-determined land uses. Inevitably, however, the usefulness of activity data is dependent on the classification applied to it and, in fact, there is little to indicate that a very sophisticated classification is likely to be any more effective than one of a simpler type. Once grouped, activity types can be analysed to determine resource and user requirements. The resource requirements will be of immediate significance in generating a spectrum of activities which the site is physically capable of sustaining to some degree: participant requirements become increasingly relevant in the subsequent evaluation of alternative activities.

Rarely will a site be devoid of any recreational potential. In general, therefore, comprehensive development of the site should be designed to secure the optimum exploitation of the initial potential. The intensity of use to which a site may be subject is defined by its ability to accommodate visitors within any predetermined management constraints. In modifying any absolute measures of site carrying capacity by incorporating management policies, we arrive at the notion of planned site capacity and the associated phenomenon of 'peaking' to which every form of recreation is susceptible in one form or another. This will be considered further in relation to management planning.

# CHAPTER SEVEN

# *Management Planning*

In coming to a decision about the establishment of a recreational enterprise in either the public or the private spheres, account must be taken of
a wide variety of relevant facts and situations. These are probably not
fundamentally different from those which face the initiator of any new
venture, whether in town or country, and a path will have to be cut
through them. In this process of decision-making the instigator will be
moulding his management model. He will be defining, and perhaps modifying, his management objectives, so that they may, at the end, look
somewhat different from those with which he began. In many cases
there will emerge a simple objective, such as that of maximizing profits,
which will be set within a ring of constraints; some of these may have
been formulated during the decision-making process, others may have
been imposed on the grant of planning permissions, others by bylaw,
building regulation and sanitary requirements. Whether the management
model is moulded or the objective defined within a ring of constraints
the process does not only take place between the sowing of the idea and
its eventual flowering, but continues during the whole period over which
the enterprise is in being. It is, however, essential that any alteration of
objectives is gradual once the final decision to go ahead is in the process
of realization, lest management and financial chaos result.

The process of allocating resources to achieve particular ends in an
explicit fashion identifies the role of management planning. Once the
purposes for which the enterprises are established have been fully
defined (and ideally such a decision should be come to in consultation
with the management organization if it is yet in existence), then management policies can be selected to achieve them. If possible these policies
should not be left to take shape after the design-team has completed
its work, for in the running of a recreational enterprise which will have

to cater for a large number of people some of the processes of management control will depend upon the design and layout of the site. It may not always be possible to ensure that design and management work in concert and the management team may be presented with a site design and layout already in being. In such a case there is every chance that in one or more respects the management organization will criticize the layout with which it is presented. However, should the management change after the enterprise has already started, any new manager is almost certain to do the same. To appoint the manager before the project is ready to work may, at first sight, appear to be a waste of money, but this depends upon the complexity of the site and upon the total investment in relation to which a year's salary for the manager may well be negligible — and ultimately more than worth spending.

At this point in the narrative it must be acknowledged that the management functions of the public and the private sectors are somewhat different. In the private sector any one proprietor is usually dealing with only a single recreational enterprise (however complex) and needs to set up a management organization for it. In the public sector, however, the provision of recreation may be a general function of the county or district council over a wide area. The council may provide or encourage recreational facilities in its area, to do which it must adopt a broad policy (e.g. whether to be active in the provision of sites or not) and that policy will be made in the political sphere. Beneath that lies the more detailed implementation policy and beneath that again will lie the management objectives of the individual sites as they are eventually selected. There may, therefore, be levels of management in the public sector which do not normally appear in the private sector and in the private sector there are levels of business management with which many portions of the public sector do not deal. This is, of course, a generalization. The point is that where an enterprise is run on a commercial basis (most private recreational enterprises are, many public recreational enterprises are not), then detailed business management is involved. Where recreational policy lies with elected representatives, it is in the political sphere and must be translated into practice through the permanent officials of the council concerned. That practice will involve both broad sector planning (e.g. decisions on the areas in which recreational enterprises are to be provided) and detailed use and site planning once the recreational areas have been acquired. Beyond this stage again active management is involved, but here the management will be of a number of recreational sites, both large (as country parks) and small (as picnic areas) and the elected representatives will not be involved in the running of each area. There will have to be devised a management organization, which may simply be a warden in charge of each site or of a number of sites, with a labour force to do the work on the ground. Where, however, a public sector park is either of itself complex, or commercially run, a special management organization will have to be set up to deal with that site itself (cf. the Wirral Country Park in Cheshire or the Queen Elizabeth and Butser Hill Country Parks in Hampshire). Almost every authority deals with this problem differently. In each case however, management objectives must be defined within which a manager can formulate a policy.

In the private sector one is dealing with the broad problem on a smaller scale. A decision on the establishment of, say, a country park, once made and implemented, is left behind. It will probably never have to be made again. The objectives can be laid down and, although subject to change over time, relate usually to a single site. Management then takes on and formulates a policy through which the objectives may be realized and is involved at once in the implementation of that policy. Depending upon the size of the organization, day to day running may be delegated to a specific site manager, or, if the organization and the enterprise is small, to a warden or departmental head who will run the enterprise as one of the estate departments with a responsibility back up the chain of management to the owner.

In the majority of cases, in both the public and private spheres, the first constraint facing the entrepreneur is the fact that he has not got absolute freedom of choice of the area within which an enterprise is to be established, nor, within that area, freedom of choice of the site. In the private sphere the entrepreneur's freedom of choice is probably more severely limited than in the public sphere, for, as a landowner, he will be looking only to land over which he can already exercise some control (i.e. he is not looking to acquire land far beyond the borders of his present ownership, if indeed he is looking to acquire land at all). In the public sphere, however, a decision may be made on the area in which an enterprise might beneficially be set up and the area then searched for an appropriate site. Potentially, having compulsory powers, the public authority has a much wider choice than the individual: but however wide the apparent choice, physical factors as well as the location in relation to other land and land uses, availability of services, transport, etc. will make each site unique. In practice, as has already been suggested, most sites will 'emerge' as possibilities for recreational use. However sites are selected, and they may come forward for consideration, and assessment will have to be made of the recreational and other uses to which they might be put. No doubt the assessor, in his role of entrepreneur, will have a preconceived idea of the main type of recreational provision which appears to be necessary in the whole area concerned: indeed, without putting too fine a point on it, he may, for months or years, have been looking for the 'right' opportunity. Powers given to local government to provide or improve opportunities for the enjoyment of the countryside by the public should, if exercised, lead the authority to seek to assess what types of enjoyment opportunity should be provided, then to look for the area within which such provision is likely to be most used and finally to seek the site within that area where the opportunity can indeed be made available. Within the private sphere, however, the site is likely to emerge first unless an entrepreneur is, like the local authority, seeking to provide a facility and searching for a suitable site. In practice, of course, many of these processes go on at the same time and it is not always possible to be sure whether the facility precedes the site or the discovery of the site gives rise to a search for the facility.

However, whether the site has been found which will satisfy the primary recreational purpose or whether the recreational use has to be decided in relation to an available site, it will be necessary to come to a considered opinion on the uses to which the site could be put. While this assessment may in many cases be directed solely towards potential recreational use, nevertheless such use is, perhaps, only one of a number of choices and only when the recreational potential can be set alongside the potential for other uses can the final decision be arrived at. This thesis emphasizes again the different measures of assessment which may be used in the public and the private sphere — perhaps to the detriment of the private? In the latter a clear measure in the first instance is the financial profitability of the various choices; in the former social benefit may stand to be measured against social benefit or, with more difficulty, against financial gain. For example, the single owner can simply measure the capital costs, running costs and annual income to which one type of use may give rise against those of other uses and employ the valuation techniques of discounted cash flow to compare the results. While these may not dictate the final decision, which could still be come to on a subjective judgment, they will at the least make it possible for the decision-maker to acknowledge that there are other things than the degree of financial success which should be weighed in the balance. Where, however, in the public sphere, obvious like cannot be compared with obvious like (for a recreational use not run with a view to the realization of profits cannot be directly compared with other uses which are, e.g. farming or forestry), then there would seem to be no common basis from which to make further subjective judgments.

The allocation of land to specific uses is one of the primary decision—making responsibilities of the land manager, and if this is to be carried out in a rational manner he must be aware of the areas of knowledge which will improve the objectivity of his decisions: in particular, the value of the resources available to him and the patterns of demand affecting land utilization. Value is the yardstick of all management. Managers of similar organizations tend to adopt conventionalized measures of value (often financial) as much as anything else to facilitate comparison of management performance among other things. So often, however, in dealing with countryside recreation we are talking about employing resources which may in every sense be unique. In this case the manager will be obliged to assign to such resources values which are inherently subjective. Nevertheless he should make some attempt to underwrite those values with a more objective evaluation of the resources possibly using an opportunity-cost measure which would by implication restore an element of comparability to the otherwise oversubjective assessment. Demand must be capable of expression in terms of land requirements at a site level. Whereas a land-use planner may attempt to equate effective demand with overall demand, e.g. by assessing applications for planning permission in the light of planning policies, at the site level the manager is capable of imposing his own tight control on effective demand, though attempts to influence overall demand may be more difficult.

'Overall demand' for recreation needs to be translated into site management terms by expressing it in terms of defined activities for which resource requirements can be readily established (see Fig. 12). The majority of known recreation activities have already been variously classified. Inevitably there are, and will continue to be, activities instigated as a result of the imagination and originality of the intuitive entrepreneur. His ideas may be largely unsubstantiated in objective terms; indeed many successful enterprises have been developed simply from an original idea and the financial backing to implement it. It may also be argued that few successful innovative ideas are purely intuitive — they are likely to be based on some experience, research and analysis (though it may be unsystematic). Knowledge of known enterprises cannot, therefore, be ignored and may, indeed, generate originality when known alternatives

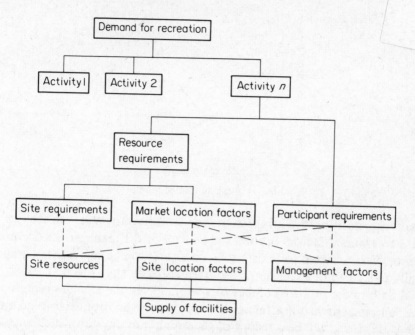

Fig. 12. Determinants of recreational land use.

fail to meet management objectives. New enterprises, original or not, can be objectively evolved in a systematic manner.

Where for one reason or another the land manager is concerned that the recreational potential of a particular site requires further investigation, this process should be aimed at assessing how the initial potential of the site can best be exploited. When factors relating to location, access and demand are considered constant, for a given level of management the number of visits to the site will be dependent on the properties of the site and of competing sites – this being largely beyond the control of the manager. In adopting this simplified approach, the manager can concentrate his planning on the capcity of the site to carry visitors. From day to day the carrying capacity of any site is inevitably a constantly varying factor but here we are talking about planning, not running, the enterprise: the rational manager is, therefore, concerned with standards or targets. The normative concept of planned site capacity will help him in objectively considering capacity 'standards'.

One of the major imponderables faced in establishing site capacity standards is the phenomenon of 'peaking' – or fluctuations in visitor attendance – which must be taken into account. Although 'peaking'

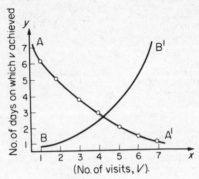

Fig. 13 Site attendance graph

manifests itself on-site it represents in part a sensitivity in site attend-ance to external factors beyond the control of the manager. Its occur-rence can be charted for existing facilities and can be represented graph-ically in a curve of exceedance for attendance on site (Fig. 13).

A daily record of the number of visitors yields the $x$-values representing the full range of visitor attendances over the season. For each value on the $x$-axis there will be a record of the number of days on which any given figure was achieved — represented on the $y$-axis. A curve such as $AA^1$ showing high numbers of visitors on just a few days implies that a substantial degree of peaking occurs; a curve such as $BB^1$, on the other hand, shows high numbers achieved on most days and low numbers only occasionally — a negative peaking. Of course, the values involved will vary from site to site and from season to season, but plots for successive seasons will allow a mean curve to be constructed. For new sites the curve of exceedance will not be a product of monitoring, but of forecast-ing site attendances on the basis of comparable information from else-where. Whatever the basis upon which the graph is founded, what is evolved is a curve of exceedance for the normative year in the planned life of the enterprise.

The next step is to use the curve to yield that figure of daily visitor attendance upon which development plans will be based. The selection of the visitor attendance/site capacity figure will be determined by the manager in accordance with his objectives. Before considering the main criteria which might influence his decision, it is as well to point out first that in deciding on one point of a curve, the slope of the curve at that point will give the manager an idea of the sensitivity of his choice. Furthermore, if little peaking occurs and an enterprise is running close to its limiting capacity, the $BB^1$ curve may reduce in length and increase the possible margin of error in analysing a small section of it; and under such conditions 'visual' analysis may have to give way to algebraic analysis based on differential calculus.

There are three primary criteria — technical, social and economic — which the manager applies explicitly to fix his attitude towards planned site capacity; these attitudes are likely to become the foundation of admission policy for the site and explicitness is, therefore, essential. Physical constraints will impose technical criteria which may range from the physical or ecological capacity of the site to the capacity and efficiency of an on-site transport system. So far as ecological capacity is concerned, the previously mentioned stage of site-resource evaluation should have yielded a measure of the level of use which resource components could be expected to sustain without unacceptable physical deterioration. Social criteria will be influenced by the desire to make the site easily available for as wide a spectrum of visitors as possible. One would expect a difference in attitude here between public and private sector management. Although, ultimately, financial cost will limit freedom of use, there will be a less determinate intermediate stage of deciding on the number of days upon which visitors should be refused access to the site. As first mentioned there are few sites where financial constraints are non-existent. These will normally be determined by reference to the expected benefits and associated costs of providing and running the facilities, but again the basis upon which expected benefits in particular will be assessed will differ in accordance with the objectives of the owner or controller of the site.

Once the daily attendance figure upon which the operating capacity of the site is to be based has been established, a closer look at this figure is required. The daily figure does not necessarily represent the number of people actually on the site at any given moment in the day: visitors enter and visitors leave creating a state of flux. What the manager needs to know is the maximum number of visitors actually on-site during the day — i.e. the difference between the number entering the site and the number having already left (Fig. 14). The maximum point on the momentary average-attendance curve signifies the maximum number of visitors on-site any time during the day and the time at which that peak is reached. The daily pattern of visitor attendance is obviously valuable in planning the staffing requirements of the site but, of more general importance, the maximum momentary average attendance on the normative day provides a reference datum for the planned capacity of the site.

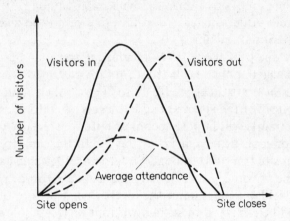

Fig. 14 Daily average attendance graph

The actual method just described of determining a planned capacity level is in itself simple: the major difficulty inherent in its use as a fore-casting technique on a planned site lies in obtaining comparable data on which to construct the curves described. Apart from the inherent unique-ness of sites from which comparable evidence is to be obtained, unless the requisite data is to be specially obtained, there are the problems of its amalgamation from sources with non-standardized recording proce-dures. In other words, this technique must simply be viewed as an aid to planning. However, once the site is established the method, unlike many forecasting techniques, becomes more rather than less useful in forming a basis for the monitoring of the site: the manager immediately has a yardstick against which management may be evaluated in a rudi-mentary way.

From a general consideration of site capacity, we come to the question of detailed site-planning. There is no technique to apply to a site in order to assess its potential recreational use as precise as the techniques which the expert can apply to a choice of farming enterprises or to the choice of tree species suitable for an area of woodland, for recreation provides services, not goods. These services are the provision of entertainment. The consumer's preference for entertainment is fickle, uncertain and subject to change, yet a start can be made by, perhaps, listing every potential recreational use for which a particular site might be suitable and not eliminating any one because of its incompatability with others. In compiling such a list, the planner may have before him a template as suggested by the Sports Council and the Countryside Commission. This in fact, provides a long list of recreational uses to which 'any' site might be put.

Figure 12 shows how detailed land-use decisions may be primarily activity-determined or supply-determined. Armed with his resource analysis and an 'activity list' the manager could, theoretically, consider both sources equally and fully, but to do so would produce a cumbersome range of choices thus making subsequent selection tedious and overcomplicated. There is likely to be an intuitive tendency to favour one of these two determinants, leaving the other in the position of a constraint filtering out the remoter extremes of the 'theoretically possible' range of enterprises. The process of reducing the complete spectrum of enterprise possibilities introduces the need to evaluate the choices available to the manager, this being the first step in the selection procedure which will ultimately lead to the distillation of the preferred enterprise mix.

Without doubt an activity list is a handy tool. It gives the planner the opportunity, without undue thought, to apply appropriate uses to the site he is investigating, enabling him at the same time to eliminate the clearly impossible (e.g. mountaineering in the fens) and the unsuitable (e.g. parachuting into woodlands) so that his list is reduced to one of containable size. A pre-prepared list has one particular disadvantage, namely, the temptation it carries with it for the planner to eliminate not only suggested uses, but also individual thought and inspiration. The possible uses thus suggested can now be looked at as applied to the site with a view to deciding not only the extent of their suitability, but also how far they would content with each other, either physically (e.g. sailors and water-skiers cannot use the same piece of water at the same time) or financially (e.g. the money available for development is limited or two uses may mutually exclude each other because they would both satisfy the same demand and thus compete with each other). A variety of uses might, on the other hand, be run on different parts of the same site attracting different sections of the public but to the extent that the physical capacity of the car parks, roadways and entrances could not cope with the simultaneous demand. Other uses might be mutually exclusive because the one would preclude the full enjoyment of the other by reason, for example, of noise or other disturbance. Such considerations will enable the planner to prune his list; in doing this, however, he must remember that while one mixture of uses will enable him to eliminate certain other uses a different mixture may bring some back on to the list again. It is not, however, as complicated as it sounds, for in most cases the list of truly possible uses is comparatively small and

the effect of interuse-swapping not impossible to determine. In many
cases also there will be an obviously predominant use to which ancillary
uses will be subordinate, or an obviously predominant resource (e.g. a
large lake) which will again dictate the extent of ancillary uses. Even when
the list has been shortened to one containing really possible uses not incompatible with one another, their interplay will have to be considered.
For instance, the pattern of movement which a use will impose on the
site can be shown on a plan (and, indeed, possibly the timing of that
pattern) and by the use of overlay plans movement-time patterns which
impinge on one another can be made manifest. Such patterns could
dictate uses at this stage of the exercise. Such patterns will certainly
dictate layout and management plans at a later stage of the development
process.

Up to now there has been a presumption that the manager in seeking
to identify a preferred combination of enterprises, has been working from
a spectrum of possible activities which he has already developed. It is
conceivable, however, that if a premium is placed on innovative management, then as a matter of predetermined policy all or most of a spectrum
of readily identifiable choices may be rejected because of the ease with
which they have been identified. The innovative manager could actively
be seeking enterprises beyond the scope of any 'standard' list of choices.
The normative approach to enterprise selection may also endanger the
possibility of incorporating a fortuitous, unforeseen enterprise – where,
for example, the manager has an opportunity to introduce an original
enterprise resulting from an entrepreneurial initiative.

Nevertheless the manager should now possess a comprehensive idea
of potential management  of choices including (a) those which will be
immediately acceptable in relation to available resources and the forecast demand to which they would be subject; (b) others which are
potentially suitable subject to the acceptability of conditions which may
be functions of internal management conditions, e.g. the agressiveness
of the marketing policy to be pursued. The first stage of selection from
this range of potentially acceptable choices comprises the evaluation
of each one to assess (a) its individual potential contribution to the
recreational management plan, and (b) its potential collective contribution to that plan. Evaluation places a responsibility on the manager to
assess, objectively, the potential contribution of any management
choice. Inability to do this should not, *prima facie,* constitute a criterion
for rejection.

Enterprise evaluation within rural estate management is generally synonymous with financial evaluation of enterprises. In relation to the full gamut of recreation activities and facilities complete financial evaluation of every enterprise is unnecessary. It is demanding of management resources in relation to the length and complexity of the evaluation process and to the amount of enterprise data to be assembled from elsewhere which may not be freely available from independent or centralized sources. Much of the financial data which can be assembled will be made redundant as the selection procedure develops. Furthermore, simple evaluation of individual enterprises is likely to be potentially misleading when combinations of activities are assembled to constitute the complete recreation enterprise. At this stage, therefore, other evaluation factors are more appropriate than financial analysis.

Unlike agriculture, where financial yardstick of performance for every enterprise have been developed over the past 20 years or so, 'mass' recreation is, generally, too recent a phenomenon to have permitted the development of management yardsticks over a similar period. As stated previously, the element of individuality and choice implicitly associated with recreation suggests that yardsticks which could plausibly be applied to enterprise performance are likely to be of the most rudimentary nature. None the less two primary indices do suggest themselves as contributing to systematic evaluation: these are (a) an individual index, and (b) a complementary index. The individual index reflects the contribution which each element of the enterprise is capable of generating in isolation, while the complementary index reflects the complementary nature of many activities or enterprise elements which in combination with others produce a greater collective output or benefit than would otherwise have been expected.

The potential contribution of the individual activity may be evaluated in accordance with the following parameters:

(1) Inherent attraction, i.e. the capacity of the activity to draw people to it without coercion. The generation of visitors does presuppose their awareness of the activity but this awareness may be instilled by information rather than by more active encouragement.

(2) Participatory attraction — the capacity of the activity to involve people in its consumption over and above mere passive involvement.

(3) Uniqueness or more precisely the sensitivity of consumption to the availability of substitute facilities. This factor implies awareness on the part of the management of the pattern of provision of recreation facilities in the neighbourhood as well as the determinants of demand and the specific requirements of potential participants.

(4) Reliance on external factors such as staturory requirements for development, construction, etc.

(5) Resource requirements — the demand which the activity is likely to place on estate resources; land, labour, capital or enterprise.

How different facilities affect each other may, however, be judged in accordance with the following priorities. First, an 'ancillary factor': some activities and facilities tend to be considered as being ancillary to other activities but none the less essential to the efficient functioning of the primary activity. Often these 'service' facilities providing basic visitor needs can be separately identified in which case their main benefit may be of a complementary but identifiable nature to other primary activities. This factor is associated with the mutual interdependence of activities. Second, corresponding to the notion of increased collective output, there is a participation attraction factor to represent activities which in themselves may be insignificant in acting as a primary generator of site attendance but given a 'captive' market may be capable of generating considerable benefit to the recreation enterprise as a whole, e.g. 'amusements', souvenir shops. Again resource requirements and reliance on external factors must be taken into account in determining the index.

Inevitably the transition from the range of choices, through evaluation to the final selection stage presupposes the application of management judgements and values. The individual and complementary indices will comprise several contributory factors which, unless they have equal significance, will require 'weighting' to reflect their relative importance. Such weightings will be determined in accordance with management policy, judgment and 'style' and will be dependent on the preferences of the management. Nevertheless the evaluatory function of the two indices reduces the total spectrum of choices to a smaller range evolved by applying broad management values to the original range. Once the manager has identified the key factors which determine the potential of any given activity for a specific site and for specific management requirements, he may then attempt to identify the sensitivity of those factors to prevailing management conditions and requirements. Although this may, in reality, be on subjective grounds, it does at least provide a systematic procedure for the initial appraisal of the range of choices available to the manager. It must also be remembered that once an enterprise is established and monitored data becomes available, this evaluation procedure can be modified by statistical analysis. At the

innovation stage the state of knowledge and the difficulty in applying site-specific data to new situations render techniques such as factor
analysis or principal component analysis unproductive. Furthermore, the
intuitive nature of innovative management means that a dogmatic discussion of the weightings which could be attached to these factors is
meaningless, since the weightings will be derived from the individual
utility concepts of the manager.

Thus, gradually, the sifting will be done. However, a major mesh in the
sieve not yet fully encountered will be financial considerations. In the
public sphere, in most cases, the financial sieve will be concerned with
capital and running costs and probably only to a minor extent with the
income which the enterprise may be expected to generate. Time and circumstances alter cases and revenue may become an important element
in the future: but whether it will be or not is as much a political decision
as a financial one.

In the private sphere capital costs will almost certainly be subject
to assessment in the light of the return expected (i.e. income less
expenditure). Here it is often hard to assess the amount of income which
a particular use may generate, for the success of a recreational enterprise
depends largely upon the total experience gained by those who are
attracted to it; the proportion of an entrance fee attributable to any
single attraction within the ring fence is hard to predict beforehand.
Where separate charges are made for different activities, then guesses
beforehand may be translated into facts afterwards (which may be too
late!). Here the experience of long-established enterprises which carefully monitor their successes or failures could well be useful. However,
it is worth repeating a cautionary note here for the unwary. Although
monitoring systems will be considered in greater detail later on, a major
contribution of monitoring data is in the development of measures of
financial performance. Their use as management yardsticks is largely
confined to the site on which they have been obtained because of the
sensitivity of such figures to site and management characteristics.
Consequently their validity in application to other sites must be carefully
assessed. Furthermore, there is no conventionalized basis (such as exists
for the financial analysis of agricultural enterprises) to enable such
yardsticks to be uniformly or systematically developed for recreation
enterprises (i.e. apart from general conventions of 'management'
accounting).

The appraisal of a new enterprise or activity will be concerned, essentially, with the net benefit capable of being generated by the activity, and ideally the marginal benefit of the activity, although the magnitude of the resource components of an activity may render marginal analysis impracticable. There appears to be a tendency to associate the derivation of social benefit (assuming this is not a spurious objective) with the exploitation of natural resource potential and a presumption that this is linked to implicit preference. If so, this would tend to give rise to a cost-minimizing approach to the evaluation problem while the derivation of financial benefit would be more likely to stem from a benefit-maximizing approach.

Two of the principal components of the selection problem consist of (1) forecasting potential revenue, and (2) estimating the cost of deriving that revenue. The first of these is a variable factor initially dependent on management policy. Initially, however, consideration of the financial aspects of either consumption or cost will be governed by the sensitivity of potential output to other factors. Once the manager can identify the sensitive elements determining the profitability of an enterprise, he can isolate the activities which are likely to have lowest potential benefit when assessed in the light of management values.

In calculating costs in the public or private sphere the availability of Exchequer grants made by the Minister, usually through the medium of the Countryside Commission, will have to be taken into account. The Countryside Act deals with such grants in several of its sections. Under the Act grants to local authorities may not exceed 75 per cent of the expenditure in respect of which the grants are made (and in practice do not, in fact, exceed 50 per cent in most cases). Grants or loans may be made also to persons other than public bodies who carry out approved projects, and again the upper limit fixed by the Act is 75 per cent of the expenditure in respect of which the grant is made. In every case conditions may be attached when a grant or loan is made. These points are dealt with in more detail in Chapter 3 on the Countryside Commission.

The costing of development proposals is a relatively technical process and may be viewed as part of the sieving involved in the primary stages of evaluation. The preliminary evaluation is essentially negative in character, getting rid of activities which are manifestly inappropriate and which will not foreseeably be adopted. The final selection procedure is, on the other hand, essentially positive in nature: its object is to synthesize appropriate strategies for implementation. Here the manager must reflect the utility functions of those concerned with his management policies. In some instances these will be concerned with securing financial benefits, in other cases the benefits will be social. However, it is beyond the scope of this present text to enter detailed discussion of the techniques of capital budgeting or the evaluation of social benefit.

It is not easy to pick the point in the development of a recreational enterprise at which the management plan can be said to begin for, as pointed out above, the whole process of development is a continuing one which starts with the idea and the opportunity which merges into realization and of which management is a part. The management plan, even when only in embryo, is an element in the development plan, for as the design of management will depend upon the shape and process of development so will the shape and process of development depend to an extent upon the management resources available (as it must depend upon the financial resources available).

In essence a management plan is the same sort of vehicle whether it is being prepared for use in the public or private sphere, except that in the private sphere there is probably one extra element of the plan which is the decision on the nature of the enterprise ownership. In discussing the essential elements of the management plan below, therefore, this element is included, with the realization that it is probably inappropriate in the preparation of a plan in the public sector. In any given case other elements of the following management plan 'checklist' may be inapplicable; furthermore, it must be acknowledged that the order of the items in the checklist may not be in a correct order of priority in every case.

In considering the preparation of a management plan, therefore, it must be appreciated that there are elements in the following outline which will be inappropriate in any given case in either the public or private spheres and, further, that there is not necessarily any precise point at which the plan must begin. What, after all, is a management plan? In the simplest sense it is a plan under the guidance of which a particular enterprise will be run. But where in this context does management begin, and is one dealing only with physical management, the number, grades and responsibilities of the staff, the pattern of visitor management, the arrangements by which the fixed equipment is repaired and the area kept clean, or also with financial management and control which will include not only the keeping of adequate records and accounts, but also the structure of ownership under which the enterprise is to be run? There are, indeed, grades and degrees of management planning which might be broken down into the periods of time covered by various activities or identified in rather the same way as capital is distinguished from revenue. For example, as far as physical management is concerned, the capital element might be that which takes shape over the development period, and it is difficult sometimes to distinguish management in this sphere from planning. A part, also, of the capital element would be that sphere of management which deals with the ownership structure of the enterprise. A comprehensive management plan (or perhpas development report?) will take the entrepreneur through these development and layout considerations and will present him with a plan which, upon implementation, will involve physical factors like the layout of the site, the making of paths and roads and car parks, the planting of trees and shrubs and the erection of buildings. But, as has been said before, it should not be possible to complete the physical planning of the area (let alone its implementation) unless at the same time thought has been given to the way in which the layout will affect day to day running. Further, where grant aid is being sought from the Countryside Commission, the management plan which they are likely to require to be submitted with the grant application is bound to be concerned with the shape, design and siting of the buildings and facilities towards the cost of which they are being asked to contribute, as well as with the details of how they are to be run when they are up. Ownership structure may not, on the other hand, necessarily be of invariable concern to the Commission nor perhaps to a local authority where no ownership choice is available anyway. In providing a checklist for a management plan, therefore, the authors acknowledge that it is both a shot in the twilight and something which in any given circumstance may be partially, if not wholly, inappropriate.

## THE MANAGEMENT PLAN

As stated above, the point in the development process at which a mangement plan can effectively be presented is not easily identified. The outline given below begins where the main development proposals have been formulated, on the argument that it is only then that there is anything to manage. In essence the plan will be a written document, supported by as many maps or diagrams as may be necessary and it is suggested that it may take the following form:

**Introduction:** The first steps in explaining the plan are to describe briefly the site itself and the area in which it is situated; making reference to the hinterland from which the probable users will be drawn and to the population within it, so that the basis of the asseement of the number of people likely to use the facilities is clear. It will then be necessary to define and rank the objectives of the plan and the constraints applied in their achievement. These constraints may be geographical, physical and ecological and imposed by the area in which the site lies and by the conformation and aspect of the site itself (and thus largely immutable). Or they may be legal or they may be social and financial, imposed by the body or owner under whose authority the development is being carried out (and thus not necessarily impossible to modify); or they may be constraints which have emerged during the consideration of the development plan – in which case they may change if the plan itself changes.

**Implementation of objectives:** The plan should next describe the way in which the objectives already referred to are to be implemented by setting out the uses to which it is proposed the site should be put, where particular facilities are to be situated and which are to be the main and subsidiary uses. In this section reference could also be made to any proposals which envisage the holding of special events from time to time. Reference could be made here to the positive banning of specific uses which affect management. Prohibition of certain types of use may have already been referred to in the introduction under the heading of 'constraints'. Under 'implementation', however, the intention is to point out those activities, both positive and negative, which may have a direct impact on management. It is, for example, one thing not to provide facilities for a specific use yet quite another actively to prohibit it. In the former case nothing has to be done, in the latter extensive wardening or the erection and maintenance of physical barriers may be necessary.

Having described the uses (or prohibitions) which will entail management – and these uses may or may not be separately charged for – it is now necessary to describe the services which will be provided complementary to those uses or to the general use of the area, which themselves will impinge on the management organization; such as access, car parks, egress, and the provision of interpretation services, children's play areas, lavatories, on-site transport for visitors and the like. By the end of the implementation section, there should have been built up a full picture of the enterprise for which management will be necessary.

It could be argued that the implementation section should examine in detail the major uses and services to be provided so that their management can later be discussed. This is a matter for judgment in any given case. Here, however, it is suggested that 'implementation' should be completed before 'management' begins and that the proper place to consider the details of the uses is in the section dealing with management, because management depends on use and use dictates management and the two cannot properly be separated.

**Management:** With the completion of the previous section, which describes the activities and constraints to which management will be devoted, the management team itself may now be examined. It is suggested that there may, for any given recreational enterprise, be three levels of management, namely, overall management (including ultimate financial management), enterprise management and site management or control. Overall management may, as suggested earlier, be undertaken in the public or large-scale sphere by an organization responsible for a wide variety of enterprises (e.g. by a county recreation department) or in the smaller context, by a controller working with the owner or as a membrer of a high-level board through the agency of which policy decisions are taken. Although, as between the public and private spheres, the top-level organization will vary, its main function will not. Depending upon the size of the total recreational venture and relative to the site in question, there may be imposed an enterprise manager who will have a duty towards the whole complex. He, or she, will be, in particular, responsible for the integration of the various activities and uses on the site, for overseeing individual departmental heads (where there are such) and for ultimate control. Within the immediate responsibility of the manager may lie day to day financial management, publicity and promotion. In the line of responsibility there may next be placed heads of departments whose duty will be the efficient functioning of the various special uses within the whole recreational enterprise (e.g. interpretation, museum, house-opening, restaurant, sailing, garden-centre, etc.). To each of these will be allocated the necessary staff. Apart and aside from the departmental organization it may well prove necessary to provide some sort of a wardening service, a cleaning and maintenance team and persons to control traffic and car-parking. Great skill lies in the construction and organization of the management team, the size of which tends to increase at the smallest opportunity. It must be realized that one man can in fact do many jobs and that in a number of instances, where, for example, a recreational area is a true country park and not an entertainments centre, a single warden with or without occasional help can function efficiently. Within the management section of the plan it will be necessary to include reference to concessionaires and the terms and conditions upon which they may be allowed to operate, and to the organization and running of specific sections of the total enterprise such as interpretation centres, children's play areas or adventure playgrounds, nature walks and the like.

**Finance**: The management plan must, of course, be concerned with finance but the detail will greatly depend upon the enterprise for which the plan is being drawn up. If a development plan has been prepared in detail before the management plan, then capital expenditure and its spread will have already been decided upon. If, however, the development plan merely outlines the development proposals and perhaps prices them overall, the management plan must be concerned with the implementation of the development plan and its timing; especially so if development is to be spread over a number of years. The management plan should separate the provision and application of capital on the one hand from revenue expenditure and income on the other. The assessment of probable capital expenditure (inflation apart) on the establishment of an enterprise is not too difficult an exercise, but the calculation of the annual income likely to be earned from a venture which is not yet running can only be based on a pilot study or on the experience of others and will rarely be anything other than speculative. Of course, once a year's actual figures are to hand, the guesses become more accurate as a result of careful monitoring. At any given level of management, however, certain of the annual expenditure forecasts can, from the outset, be reasonably accurate though others must depend upon attendance numbers. From the point of view of a management plan some financial predictions of capital expenditure and of annual income and outgoings are obviously necessary. In the public sphere, in the case of a non-commercial enterprise, fairly accurate figures can be submitted, though their accuracy lessens as the period over which they are calculated lengthens. Where such inaccuracy can be attributed to inflation, the rate of which cannot be determined in advance, there is little that the forecaster can do about it but draw his readers' attention to the problem.

In any sphere inflation will bedevil figures and, where inflationary error is compounded by an inaccurate forecast of admission numbers, the results could be so wrong as to be valueless: the trouble here, of course, is that investment decisions may have been made upon the evidence provided by these incorrect figures, and with this possibility in mind the forecaster should be careful to expunge optimism from his financial thinking and the entrepreneur careful to keep his capital expenditure down as far as possible in the initial stages. Trouble lies, indeed, on both sides of his path. On the one side excessive expenditure (particularly dangerous when undertaken with borrowed money), and on the other such restricted expenditure that the venture is strangled at birth.

From the point of view of the management plan, a careful forecast of income and expenditure is essential in order that the manager responsible for finance can assess the cash flows of the enterprise over the period concerned and thus provide for the necessary working capital, and in order also that there is an informative document which can be presented to potential lenders. In the private sphere tax will bedevil every calculation.

In a cash-flow calculation it may be considered necessary to include in the one state both capital and income flows; but one should remember that if shown separately they can always be combined afterwards, whereas if capital and revenue expenditure are added in together, it is not always easy to disentangle them later.

Where there are different policies to choose from which envisage the laying out of capital at different times and in respect of which a different pattern of income and expenditure flows will emerge, the discounted cash-flow technique may be applied to each pattern, under which future incomes and future expenditures are discounted back to the same starting-date, so that the present values of every scheme can be compared, or the return (known as the 'internal rate of return') on each calculated.

**Monitoring and control**: It may be that the author of a management plan wishes to suggest, as part of that plan, methods by which the progress of the enterprise is monitored. It is suggested that such methods should be referred to towards the end of the plan document. In many a commercial undertaking it is possible to devise, within the accounting system, standards against which current performance can be measured and these standards can, if thought necessary, be brought to bear regularly on performance (see Chapter 8). Sophistication of management accounting has not yet progressed so far as to be able to suggest national or regional standards for various types of recreational enterprise, but it is only a matter of time and patience before such standards are produced. In the meanwhile an enterprise can build up its own standards through the medium of which current and past performance can be compared.

Further monitoring techniques which may be suggested here are such as may be applied to visitor use of the facilities provided and to the habitual behaviour of visitors within the recreational area so that, again over time, a pattern can be discerned which of itself may be used in applying techniques of control and visitor and site management. A monitoring of the way people use a site should enable management to initiate remedial action towards, for example, protecting a particular area from the ravages of overuse before rather than after such overuse becomes apparent.

## ADVERTISING AND PUBLICITY

Reference in the management plan can be made to methods which may be used to advertise the enterprise and to keep it before the public eye. Advertising is a highly specialized skill and where it is to be at all extensively used the appointment of an outside advertising agency, or, within the organization, of a publicity manager, should be considered.

## OWNERSHIP STRUCTURE

As stated earlier in this chapter, the structure of ownership of a recreational enterprise may be important in the private sphere or necessarily ignored in the public sphere. A note, in the management plan, about the ownership structure, should therefore be included where it is appropriate.

As far as the ownership of the enterprise is concerned (and it should be emphasized that it is not land ownership but enterprise ownership which is being discussed), this will be important mainly from the point of view of taxation, the ownership of the assets concerned and the liability for debts (see also Chapter 8). Apart from ownership by a trust with its esoteric complications, with which this chapter is not concerned, ownership of a business may be in the hands of an individual, of a partnership or of a limited liability company.

For taxation purposes there is no difference between individual ownership and ownership by a partnership, except in so far as the income of a partnership is spread among the partners and thus overall taxation is probably less than where it all rests with one individual. Within a partnership the assets of the partnership are owned by the separate partners for capital taxation purposes in accordance with the provisions of the partnership agreement (on the assumption that there is one) or by the individual partners where they have not been placed into the partnership pool. Here, again, the partnership is not itself a taxable organization.

The position, however, is quite different where the ownership of the business is in the hands of a limited liability company, for a company is a legal entity in its own right and has a liability to tax on its transactions separate and distinct from any liability accruing to the owner of shares in the company.

A company's income, computed on normal accounting principles but refined to a figure of adjusted profits to take account of items in the accounts not admissable in them for taxation purposes, will be subject to corporation tax, not to income tax, and the capital gains made by a company are converted into the appropriate figure of chargeable gains and are then also subject to corporation tax. Where the profits of a company lie below a certain amount, corporation tax is charged at what is known as the 'small companies rate', which is less than the current full rate of the tax. A company's profits, therefore, are never subject to tax at a rate in excess of the current rate of corporation tax, whereas those of an individual, or of an individual in a partnership, being chargeable to income tax, may in fact suffer tax at a rate considerably higher than would be the case were they subject to corporation tax. The assets of a company are the property of the company; the shareholder owns shares. These are his assets. Where, then, a business is owned and run by a company, the value of that business in the form of shares may be spread among a large number of people and be transferred in convenient amounts and with comparative ease. The ability, therefore, of a company to accumulate income after tax (subject to the limited restrictions on this ability placed upon a 'close' company), and the way in which the shares in a company may be widely distributed, make the company-ownership structure worth considering in certain cases.

### SUMMARY OF MANAGEMENT PLAN

**Introduction**
Description of region and of site. Reference to drawing area and population
Objectives of management
Constraints – geographical, physical, legal, social, financial

**Implementation**
Site uses. Development proposals and use prohibitions
Special events and exhibitions. Sales points
Complementary services to be provided – access, car parks, lavatories, interpretation and information, egress.

**Managment**

Levels of management and chain of command – duties and responsibilities

Section and departmental heads – duties and responsibilities

Wardening, general and section staffing

Appointment and payment of staff

Concessionairies – policy and terms

**Finance**

Predicted income and expenditure on revenue and capital accounts

Cash-flow charts

Possible borrowing requirements

Degrees of financial responsibility of staff

Availability of grants

Taxation

**Monitoring and control**

Standards of enterprise performance

Prediction and budgeting

Use monitoring and visitor control

**Advertising and publicity**

Recommended extent

**Ownership structure**

Individual ownership

Partnerships

Companies

# CHAPTER EIGHT

# Financial Monitoring and Control

Chapter Five discussed the demand for recreation and towards the end gave the example of Nonesuch Park, where some actual testing of the market was undertaken before the serious matter of prediction began. Such market-testing may be possible where something of the recreational resource is already in existence. Where, however, no resource other than an area of unready land is available, actual market testing will not be possible. Such a situation must surely be rare. In the majority of cases, particularly in the private sphere, an 'attraction' (cf. house and gardens) usually exists and a pilot scheme involving little expenditure can be run for a year or two. Such a scheme will provide some concrete evidence of primary demand for the facilities provided and of the sector from which it springs. Prediction may then proceed on the basis described in Chapter 7 by a series of more or less informed guesses taking cognizance of the population (numbers and make-up) in the hinterland, of the attractions for which the site appears to be suitable and of other recreational provisions already in being which are serving the same area.

Any prediction of numbers must take into account the effect which the prices to be charged are likely to have in attracting or repelling potential customers. Here again assessments are up against an unquantifial restraint the degree of which will vary with the income and social class of those who are likely to come to the site. It may be that one level of charge will not inhibit attendance to any measurable extent but that double that amount may be expected to do so. Will the latter, however, halve or more than halve the numbers attending? Will it stop people spending once they are on the site, and would a smaller entrance charge ultimately result in higher expenditure per head per day? There really are no answers to these questions, because they are not as simple as they seem. Numbers attending and the amount of money the individual is prepared to spend depend not only upon charges but also, as any entrepreneur knows, on the quality and presentation of the goods and services offered. It is not, therefore, possible to present to the reader a table of charges and costs, or income and expenditure, which may be applied to any and every enterprise, but in saying this one must be aware that many commercially run attractions have figures of their own which are the result of careful analysis of visitor numbers and visitor expenditure over the years.

For instance, where the total number of visitors admitted is known, this can be the basis on which may be calculated the total income received from each visitor each day, how much the average visitor spends on each facility and what each facility costs to run per head, thus providing a figure of gross profit per head. On this basis it is then possible to say that, for example, in a particular year when total admissions were 150 000, each visitor spent 93p, of which 50p (53.7 per cent) was on the gate and 43p on all the other activities, catering taking 20.3 per cent of the total expenditure, the souvenir shop 12.6 per cent, the museum 10.2 per cent and the boating-lake 3.2 per cent. Conversely direct costs per visitor can be calculated on each enterprise and the manager made aware that expenditure on the souvenir shop amounted to 4p per visitor admitted at the entrance whereas (see above) the visitor himself spent 12.6 per cent of his total 93p outlay, namely 11.7p in that shop so that the gross profit thrown up per visitor by the souvenir shop was 7.7p. With figures of this nature available (if they can be got), predictions for another recreational enterprise of a similar nature may be formulated with some slight degree of confidence.

This sort of financial monitoring can be used to assess performance day by day or week by week and a market deviation from the norm investigated as soon as it appears. Furthermore, these checks and balances may be used as standards and as the basis of performance targets to be set for departmental heads. Income and expenditure per visitor per facility should be expressed as a percentage of the total expenditure as well as in currency terms, so that comparisons can be made undistorted by inflation.

The example of Nonesuch Park is now extended to an exercise in simple financial planning on the basis of predicted numbers and of an overall cost per head and a forecasting table prepared for study such as may be compiled before much money is spent.

In formulating this exercise the authors acknowledge, and regret, that it can be prepared in only broad terms, that it cannot be related to an

actual situation, that the changing value of money makes it misleading
to suggest that such figures can be used in any real-life exercise and
probably more importantly still, that while Nonesuch is, of course, based
upon an amalgam of many actual enterprises the story is a fiction! What
is being suggested is the construction of a simple cash-flow chart of such
a nature that the entrepreneur can get an impression of the probable
progress of his projected enterprise and, hopefully, some reassurance that
money invested in it, or borrowed towards its establishment, can earn a
good return and be repaid within a reasonable period. Detailed predictions
of the day by day or month by month cash flows may be prepared with
greater or lesser accuracy, but this chart gives a prediction of the cash flow
on a year-to-year basis and even then only in the broadest terms. For
example, interest on borrowed money is calculated here as payable at
the end of each year (whereas it may in fact be payable more frequently)
and on the total amount of borrowings at the start of the year; furthermore, the calculation of tax payable on profits has been made as simple
as possible, firstly by assuming that the enterprise is run by a company
(and so liable only to corporation tax) and, secondly, by not including
any capital allowances which might in fact be available. The use of a company structure and, therefore, of company taxation means that the highest
rate of tax chargeable will be at the main corporation tax rate (currently
52 per cent) and where the company's profit is such that the small
companies rate is charged this has been taken at 42 per cent. By using a
company the rate of tax is, by and large, known, whereas the individual
trader's tax rate depends upon more than the profitability of the particular concern being costed and is, therefore, never known in advance
with any degree of accuracy; moreover, a company by having to meet a
maximum tax rate of 52 per cent has probably more chance of being
able to repay loans than has the individual whose marginal tax rate may
be well above this figure. However, it has been acknowledged that the
company used will almost certainly be subject to the regulations
applicable to close companies and in consequence at least 50 per cent of
the income after tax is, for the purpose of this exercise, deemed to be
distributed and not available to pay off the initial loans.

In preparing the table certain facts have been assumed: the individual
in practice may well have to ascertain more and to guess others, with
greater or lesser precision, but at least the list given should alert the
reader to some of the questions he must ask himself and to some of the
problems he must solve. The assumptions for the completion of this
cash-flow chart are as follows:

(1) The enterprise is run by a close company. Corporation tax rate is 52 per cent and the small companies rate of 42 per cent is applicable where taxable income does not exceed £30 000 p.a. with a sliding scale of rates between £30 000 and £50 000.

(2) The rate of interest paid on borrowing is 15 per cent and interest is payable at the end of each year on the predicted borrowing at the start of the year. Arrangements have been made with the lender to finance losses by additional lending within (unspecified) limits.

(3) The initial investment in year 0 covers expenditure on layout and buildings and on the payment of managerial staff employed before the enterprise opens. No initial loss is, therefore, shown in year 0 as all expenditure in that year is treated as capital.

(4) Expenditure:— Capital in year 0 = total £50 000 of which £35 000 is borrowed.

NONESUCH PARK

| Year | Predicted attendance | Income per head | Gross income (£) | Expenditure analysis | | | Gross expenditure | P/L excl. interest on borrowing |
|---|---|---|---|---|---|---|---|---|
| | | | | Salaries and wages | Maintenance and repairs | Other at 16.5p per head | | |
| 1 | 40 000 | 70p | 28 000 | 35 000 | 6 000 | 6 600 | 47 600 | −19 600 |
| 2 | 55 000 | £1 | 55 000 | 35 000 | 8 000 | 9 075 | 52 075 | + 2 925 |
| 3 | 75 000 | £1 | 75 000 | 40 000 | 10 000 | 12 375 | 62 375 | +12 625 |
| 4 | 75 000 | £1 | 75 000 | 40 000 | 10 000 | 12 375 | 62 375 | +12 625 |
| 5 | 100 000 | £1 | 100 000 | 45 000 | 10 000 | 16 500 | 71 500 | +28 500 |
| 6 | 100 000 | £1 | 100 000 | 45 000 | 10 000 | 16 500 | 71 500 | +28 500 |
| 7 | 100 000 | £1 | 100 000 | 45 000 | 10 000 | 16 500 | 71 500 | +28 500 |

Fig. 15(a) Basics of cash flow chart

## NONESUCH PARK

| Year | Borrowing at start of year | Predicted visitor numbers | Gross income | Expenditure | Interest on borrowing at start of year | Net profit (+) loss (−) |
|---|---|---|---|---|---|---|
| 0 | | | | | | |
| 1 | 35 000 | 40 000 | 28 000 | 47 600 | 5 250 | −24 850 |
| 2 | 59 850 | 55 000 | 55 000 | 52 075 | −6 052 | − 6 052 |
| 3 | 65 902 | 75 000 | 75 000 | 62 375 | 9 885 | + 2 740 |
| 4 | 63 162 | 75 000 | 75 000 | 62 375 | 9 474 | 3 151 |
| 5 | 60 011 | 100 000 | 100 000 | 71 500 | 9 001 | 19 499 |
| 6 | 40 512 | 100 000 | 100 000 | 71 500 | 6 076 | 22 424 |
| 7 | 32 852 | 100 000 | 100 000 | 71 500 | 4 928 | 23 572 |

Fig. 15(b) Basics of cash flow chart

| Year | Taxation | | | | Balance after tax | Cash used or distributed | Repaid (+) or add to borrowing (−) | Borrowing at end of year |
| | Tax due on for year | Tax relief due on for year | Tax due | Relief c/fd | | | | |
| --- | --- | --- | --- | --- | --- | --- | --- | --- |
| 0 | | | | | | | | 35 000 |
| 1 | – | 24 850 | – | 24 850 | | | −24 850 | 59 850 |
| 2 | – | 6 052 | – | 30 902 | | | – 6 052 | 65 902 |
| 3 | nil | nil | – | 28 162 | | | + 2 740 | 63 162 |
| 4 | nil | nil | – | 25 011 | | | + 3 151 | 60 011 |
| 5 | nil | nil | – | 5 512 | | | +19 499 | 40 512 |
| 6 | 16 912 | 5 512 | 7 103 | – | 15 320 | 7 660 | + 7 660 | 32 852 |
| 7 | 23 572 | – | 12 257 | – | 11 315 | 5 657 | + 5 658 | 27 194 |

Fig. 15(b) Basics of cash flow chart (*continued*)

Many different figures may be fed into this chart to give many different results. As expenditure can be controlled, to a degree, the figure for outgoings can be relied upon with greater certainty than that for predicted income. Indeed, the outcome of the chart can be altered by reducing expenditure, for example, on staffing or repairs: a higher level of income can, however, only be attained by attracting greater numbers (at what cost?) by charging more at the gate (with what result?) or by providing attractions of such a sort as will encourage the public to spend more once they are inside.

The example given shows that the loan does begin to come down fairly steadily from the end of year 4 onwards, but a loss of over £24 000 in year 1 is much more significant than a possibly mounting profit four years later and may, or even should, give cause for serious reappraisal of the initial expenditure and of the yearly outlay on the project. It would no doubt also be advisable to test the cash flow using other figures of visitor attendance and visitor expenditure, recognizing that charges imposed should not be unduly out of line with competitors' charges unless and until a standard of excellence has been obtained which justifies them.

Almost every enterprise tends to establish its own image which, once established, is difficult to alter. This is unfortunate if the image is tarnished and the expenditure has already been high. Ideally, therefore, expansion should be steady and, as far as possible, built on proven success. Predictions such as those shown in the example should properly be checked against facts as they become apparent and, where the facts then warrant it, altered.

The imprecisions inherent in a pure prediction based entirely on informed guesses may be such as to bring the whole exercise into question (less so, of course, where the figures are based on a pilot scheme) but the preparation of a chart of this kind is inherently necessary where the establishment of a business is being thought about. Indeed, the putting together of such a table will of itself be a valuable exercise.

## MANAGEMENT CONTROL

During the course of this chapter reference has been made to the analysis of visitor income and of expenditure which can be done once an enterprise is in being. In the context in which this reference was made such analyses were tentatively suggested as the basis upon which cash flow charts could be prepared when a new, or enlarged, venture was being planned. It was further suggested that analyses prepared as a result of a pilot scheme were likely to be more reliable than those which stemmed from the experience or accounts of other people. In this section of the chapter, however, consideration is given to accounting and analysis for the purpose of management control of an existing enterprise. In preparing such figures, it is essential that management decides and defines the purposes for the attainment of which control is to be exercised. This throws one back to the management plan for the whole enterprise in which the owner's objectives were set out. The function of management is to achieve those objectives subject to the constraints which will already have been noted — or which have subsequently made themselves apparent. It is easy, sometimes, for management, from the top downwards, to forget the precise purpose for which it exists and to manage for the sake of management alone! It may be, for example, that the objectives of management are, to make a profit, to enable an historic house and grounds to be maintained, to provide local employment, to enhance the natural beauty of the countryside, to provide resources for the maintenance and improvement of other land or of agricultural or forestry businesses or to achieve a number of these objectives (which are, in fact, mainly linked to the need to build up and maintain a thriving business) the attainment of which is only possible by making available to the public the sort of entertainment for which they are prepared to pay. In the public sphere, of course, profitability — in whatever worthy cause — may not be a management objective, but efficiency in providing for public enjoyment will be. Where profitability, to one end or another, is an objective (and in the private sphere it is difficult to envisage an enterprise where one of the objectives is not at the least, to break even) and where a number of different departments are run, each charging or selling separately, management will need to know more than just the profit or loss made over the whole enterprise; it will need to know how each department is doing, what contribution each makes to the whole and which appears, from the figures, worth backing or worth dropping. Once these figures are available, then considerations other than that of profitability may hold sway. Management, however, will not be exercising any truly controlling function if its decisions are based solely upon historical records of profit or loss related, perhaps, to the last complete financial year, for by then the time for effective action may have long since passed. The analysis of accounts for management purposes must, therefore, be over the shortest time possible. This could be weekly for the larger enterprise and may indeed be daily. Man is a creature of habit and crowds faced with like choices tend to choose alike. On this premise it will usually be found that whether in any one week admission numbers have been high or low the same proportion of people will tend to spend their time and money doing the same things unless and until something changes. Each enterprise, and each department within each enterprise, will therefore tend to set and maintain its own pattern and conscious effort will be needed to change it. Where such regular records are kept and studied, management can see if any particular pattern seems to be altering and ask why. At the end of each season departmental heads can examine their individual results and prepare budgets for the following season.

Week by week figures of the gross income and outgoings of each department can easily be prepared, the turnover calculated and a figure of profit or loss per department thrown up, but, of course, these figures relate entirely to the number of people who are attracted to visit the enterprise and to the proportion who visit the particular department concerned. The former number is simply obtained if entry to the complex is by ticket sold at a turnstile, but the number who, for example, come to the souvenir shop and the number who actually buy anything from it cannot be assessed without considerable difficulty. Where tickets have to be bought to enter, say, a specialist exhibition within the main complex, then further counting is easy.

The profitability of the whole enterprise will ultimately depend upon the number of people who visit it. In many instances, therefore, analysis of income and expenditure within a complex can be based upon the total numbers admitted.

It may be that such analyses can be used in the first compilation of cash flow predictions for a new enterprise, but one must be aware that the experience of one business will not necessarily be reflected in the performance of another and that, as already mentioned, the pilot scheme is a safer foundation upon which to build. In the first instance every enterprise discovers that a few people are admitted without being counted or, if counted, without being asked to pay. The number of them may, however, be so small in comparison with the whole that it may be ignored. Up to what age, for example, are children admitted free and are there many of them? Where old-age pensioners and paying children are charged less than the normal adult, or where parties are admitted at concessionary rates, if the numbers are significant (and at certain times of the year they may be; for example school parties often proliferate in the early summer) some allowance for, or special record of, them may be important.

In the second instance there will be expenses which the whole enterprise has to meet which do not vary directly with the number of visitors. For example, insurance premiums, the repair and maintenance of buildings, rates, the upkeep of gardens and the like will remain fairly constant each year whether the enterprise flourishes or fades; indeed, some expenses may have to be met whether there is an enterprise or not. Other expenses, such as the management costs themselves, are not capable of allocation to individual departments, are not directly dependent upon admissions (though they will be in the end) but are dependent entirely upon the existence of the enterprise. It is reasonable to allocate these two categories of expenditure into two categories of overheads, namely, non-enterprise overheads and enterprise overheads. How far these overheads are, at the year's end, treated as an on-cost of each department or as unallocated outgoings which affect the ultimate profit or loss, must be left to management to decide. For the purpose of comparison of one enterprise with another enterprise overheads might well be broken down to a figure per visitor admitted, and from figures such as these management 'norms' may one day be prepared.

## RECORD SHEETS

In many cases management may assemble a periodical record sheet which, in simple terms, shows the outcome of the period and how the actual figures compare with the budgeted figures and with the figures for the same period in the previous year. Where control is to be as close as this, then the periods should probably be weekly ones, for any period longer than this provides a record so historical as to preclude effective action. Naturally the record sheets will be consolidated at the end of the season so that the whole year's results can be compared with the budget and with previous years, but management may well decide that the yearly record sheet shall contain more detail than the periodical one, particularly as far as expenditure is concerned. A sample weekly record sheet for a fictitious recreational enterprise is given in Fig. 16.

Oversophistication can be self-defeating when too much energy is expended on the production of statistics. It may be that, for example, adequate control can be exercised through the daily or weekly study of figures of turnover as set against the daily or weekly records of direct expenditure and the ratio of the one to the other regularly compared. Such figures, however, may not immediately make comparable the performance of one sector of the enterprise against others, whereas a

RECORD SHEET

For week ending Sunday
(week no. — )                         19

| | | This year | Budget | Last year |
|---|---|---|---|---|
| General Admissions | No. this week | 8 645 | 9 000 | 7 976 |
| | No. cumulative from start of season | 48 859 | 47 000 | 46 213 |
| | Adult/child ratio | 1/0.61 | 1/0.5 | 1/0.54 |
| House Admissions | No. this week | 5 385 | 5 850 | 4 841 |
| | No. cumulative from start of season | 34 934 | 30 550 | 27 265 |
| | General/house admission ratio | 1/0.71 | 1/0.65 | 1/0.59 |
| Shops | £ sales this week | 1 296 | 1 260 | 957 |
| | cumulative | 5 863 | 6 110 | 6 470 |
| | per head this week (p) | 15 | 14 | 12 |
| | cumulative (p) | 12 | 13 | 14 |
| Catering | *Cafeteria* £ sale this week | 2 766 | 2 700 | 2 233 |
| | cumulative | 14 658 | 14 570 | 13 863 |
| | per head this week (p) | 32 | 30 | 28 |
| | cumulative (p) | 30 | 31 | 30 |
| Attractions | *Astroglide* takings this week (£) | 263 | 225 | 215 |
| | per head this week (p) | 3 | 2.5 | 2.7 |
| | *Fishing* value of tickets sold this week (£) | 90 | 110 | 100 |

Fig. 16 Record sheet

properly compiled record of income and expenditure per visitor admitted
will do so in that the declining or increasing popularity of one sector can
at once be seen in a changing daily pattern of visitor outlay. This pattern,
as already pointed out, may be distorted if there is a significant number
of visitors allowed free admittance (and thus perhaps not counted).
Reduced admission charges for certain categories will not affect the
pattern significantly, even if they result in greater expenditure within the
ring fence, unless the numbers admitted under such schemes are large;
it is, however, consideration of these sort of distortions which, if pushed
to excess, could result in the exasperated abandonment of the collection
and refinement of figures.

## TAXATION

In the case of an enterprise run in the private sphere by an individual, a partnership or a company the impact of taxation on the profits and how far losses may be set off against taxable income are important consider- ations. It is not intended, however, in this short section to go into details of the law.

As far as the taxation of income is concerned the measurement of the annual income derived from the enterprise is on the normal basis of the adjusted profits shown in the annual accounts. It is of significance whether the enterprise is assessed to tax under Case I of Schedule D or under Case VI of the same schedule. A Case I assessment is applied to a trade, and the normal basis on which the taxable income from the trade is computed is the profits of the taxpayer's accounting year ending in the preceding year of assessment. Not all expenses which are incurred in the course of trading are deductible, and Section 130 of the Income and Corporation Taxes Act 1970 gives a list (qualified in some cases) of those which are not; there is no list of those which are. Generally, however, any expenditure justified by commercial expediency and incurred for the purpose of enabling the trade to be carried on and be profitable is deductible, but it must not be capital expenditure (if it is, capital allowances may be available) and it must have been incurred wholly and exclusively for the purposes of the trade.

Where profits are assessed under Case I, losses may be set off against future profits in the same trade, or for a limited period and only on election, be set off against the taxpayer's other income. Where the trade is run by a partnership, the partners are liable for tax on their share of the partnership profits. Where the trade is run by a company, corpora- tion tax and not income tax is payable. In this case, while the profits will be computed on normal accounting principles, corporation tax is charged on those profits as they arose in the financial year during which they were earned. Where a company's taxable profits are below a certain amount, they will be charged to corporation tax at the current 'small companies rate'. A company's trading losses in an accounting period may be set off against future income arising from the same trade or against profits (of whatever description) of the accounting period in which the loss arose or, within defined limits, of past accounting periods.

There are cases, especially relevant perhaps in the present context to historic houses open to the public on a limited basis, where profits are not deemed to be earned in the process of a trade but instead are treated as casual profits, in the words of the relevant statute, as 'annual profits or gains not falling under any other Case of Schedule D and not charged by virtue of Schedule A, B, C or E'. Under this Case tax is charged on the full amount of the profits or gains arising in the year of assessment (i.e. on the current-year basis) the charge in effect being limited to the excess of the receipts over the expenses which were necessary to earn them. In fact the statute makes no mention of any allowance for deduction of expenses. On this basis it can be seen that when an enterprise is assessed as a trade under Case I expenses deductions are more generously allowed than when it is assessed under Case VI. Where losses are made under Case VI relief on them is available only in so far as they can be set off against other Case VI income accruing to the taxpayer in that or a subsequent year and no relief is available against the taxpayer's income from any other source.

## CAPITAL TAXATION

It is unlikely that the owner of a recreational enterprise as such will often dispose of assets of the enterprise upon which a charge to capital gains tax will arise, except where as owner of the land and buildings which are the subject-matter of the enterprise he disposes of them.

As far as capital transfer tax is concerned circumstances alter cases. If property on which a successful recreational enterprise is being run is the subject of a chargeable transfer, the calculation of the value transferred by a lifetime transfer will be the amount by which the transferor's estate has diminished in value as a result of the transfer. To this figure the open market value of the transferred property may have considerable relevance and that value may have been enhanced by the existence of the recreational enterprise. The enterprise itself may be separate from the land (e.g. be a company) and own its own assets including perhaps some element of goodwill. If the business is transferred apart from the land (if this is possible), the value of that business will be relevant to the calculation of the value transferred.

A transferrence of all assets on death will involve an assessment of the market value of the assets transferred at that time, and here again it may be necessary to distinguish between the business and the land on which it operates and to bear in mind the effect which the one can have on the value of the other. Business assets relief may be available on the recreational enterprise in particular instances.

CHAPTER NINE

# *Visitor and Site Monitoring and Control*

When all is said and done, when the owner's objectives have been formulated, the management and financial plans prepared and the recreational project launched, the immediate aim of on-the-spot management is the provision of a lasting service for the public which may be nothing greater than the opportunity for them to take air and exercise in the countryside, or nothing less than the chance to be interestingly entertained in a variety of ways. Whatever it is going to do the public will have to be made welcome, provided with at any rate the basic necessities, tea and lavatories, and the individuals who make it up given such information as they may need to enable them to enjoy the site to the full: beyond this point information may be extended towards education on the one hand, or advertisement on the other. This chapter is not concerned with education nor with commercialism, but with information and control.

In the sphere of control the manager must try to do at least three things. First, to display the site, and in the process ensure that visitors approach the various facilities in the way or by the route he has chosen (so as, for example, to minimize overcrowding and the degradation of the site), second, to prevent wear and tear by over use and, third, to exclude visitors from, or discourage them from using, certain paths or certain areas. These areas may be permanently tender (e.g. for scientific or safety reasons) or only temporarily so because, for example, they need to be given time to recover from over use or from the depredations of the climate.

Management may approach the problem of controlling people innocently, by waiting to see how the public use or damage a site before doing anything about it, or intelligently, by anticipating events and as far as possible taking the necessary protective steps before any damage

120

or misuse occurs. In practice intelligent anticipation will have to go hand in hand with innocent hesitation. At least the permanently tender areas are probably easily identified at the start and the layout of the park and of the tracks and paths modified accordingly. Both anticipation and subsequent control, however, depend upon how the visiting public may be expected to behave; this has been observed both in the field by those engaged in recreational land management and by devotees of the behavioural sciences in a variety of situations.

As he begins the process of resource and people management, the manager must cease to look at the visitor as a statistic which may give rise to, or be induced to mitigate, financial problems, but as a person, like unto himself, who has feelings, thoughts and habits, who in coming to the enterprise is seeking the satisfaction of some need or purpose but who is, none the less, susceptible to influence. Where possible the manager should attempt to assess and understand the attitude of those who come to his domain. Probably most of them, when they visit the countryside, are simply looking for some peace and tranquillity and for a change from their normal routine. They may enjoy this change in a number of ways, actively or passively, but the majority will have made their choice of venue deliberately and will have come to the particular site with some idea of what is offered: furthermore, although the manager is advised to look upon his customers as individuals, most of them will in fact have come in groups, of which the family group will predominate, so that there will be a need to provide for and control the group rather than a single person. As far as family groups go there is likely to be a wide age range within the group — parents and children of varying ages — whose ideas of recreation will differ. It will be necessary, therefore, to consider what provision may give the greatest satisfaction to the greatest number without intruding unduly upon the pleasure of the remainder. Parents on an outing are often slaves to their children and the greatest service which can be done for them is to offer some reasonably safe occupation for the children, while the parents are left free to go their own ways or at least to watch their children, idly and at leisure. Such provision may be an adventure playground or no more than grassy open space. The former will no doubt call for the attendance of admiring, even anxious, parents, the latter will provide for games-playing while the older members of the party lie on the grass.

Varieties of visitor behaviour need to be studied. They will depend upon facilities provided (how do people treat a museum, and how do they treat an open picnic-place?) and the socio-economic groups from which the visitors come. In this context it is worth noting that provision for outdoor recreation generally is made on the assumption that different social-class groups have, like different age groups, different recreational targets and, furthermore, that country parks are sought and used by the upper socio-economic groups rather than by the others.

To many people unfamiliarity with the countryside breeds apprehension a feeling of being in a wilderness not quite to be trusted. They will avoid what appears to be unpleasant or fearsome until their curiosity, interest and desire to explore overcome their apprehension and they learn more about a strange new world. Indeed apprehension, unfamiliarity and the tendency to take the easy route, particularly in the open as opposed to dark woodland, can all be used as characteristics through which control can be exercised. It is with these sorts of characteristics and patterns of behaviour that the manager must make himself familiar. For example, water, lone trees and hillocks attract, dark coniferous woodland repels. An unfamiliar shape on the skyline may become the objective of a walk and may, indeed, be used to divert attention from closer, more vulnerable areas: but the points of attraction themselves may in the end have to be protected from the depredations of the enthusiastic thousands. Most students of behaviour are now familiar with the fact that in an enclosed space people tend to choose to sit or settle by the edge rather than in the middle and consequently a picnic area with plenty of edges will give greater satisfaction to more people than a uncompromisingly open area. Indeed, the amount of edge can be increased not merely by indenting the boundary, but by planting clumps of trees or bushes in the open centre. Many people like to picnic by their cars partly, perhaps, because they do not then have to carry the picnic things far (often furniture as well as food and drink), but partly also because in the vicinity of their cars they are on familiar ground and more easily able to establish a defensible space around them.

Some people like crowds, others avoid them. The visitor to the countryside who has not come to be entertained, but rather to make his own entertainment, will probably belong to the category of crowd-avoiders, but one individual's concept of a crowded site will be very different from another's so that to the multiple of crowd-avoiders there is no single satisfaction. However, even among this group there will be a number, and probably a large number, to whom an empty site is unattractive and even perhaps a little sinister. An open site looks more crowded than one which has a degree of cover; naturally, for all those present can be seen at once. Woodland can, therefore, 'absorb' more people and still seem less crowded than a field, but the enclosed site may indeed suffer more physical degradation than the open one for the very obstacles which hide the people channel them on to well-worn paths.

Multiple use of a particular facility may promote wear. Water attracts both because of the various uses to which it may be put (sailing, rowing, fishing, etc.) which of themselves draw spectators, and because of the sense of untroubled, uncrowded peace which it gives to those who sit or walk by it; but walkers may damage the banks of a river or lake or make the footpaths muddy and unattractive. Is it necessary to tame the banks and pathways for the sake of spectators when those using the water (sailors and fishermen) may be little concerned over the presence of mud, which in any event may keep possibly unwelcome spectators away? What in this event is the primary use of the water area?

The views of practitioners on how to stop the public from spreading litter vary from centre to centre. Some there be who maintain that litter-bins or baskets must be provided, others that their presence merely encourages the deposition of rubbish somewhere on the site (and not necessarily into the receptacles) and thereby discourages the far better habit of taking litter home. It is indeed strange that visitors who will willingly carry a heavy picnic basket with them are often unwilling to carry home their rubbish afterwards in the much lighter basket. All parties, however, agree that a permanently clean site encourages the public to keep it clean — possibly through fear of ridicule as much as through appreciation of a common duty — and that a site carrying uncleared litter-bins (for whatever reason) impresses the visitor with the obvious unconcern of management and invites careless or even defiant behaviour.

The apparent (not necessarily the actual) attitude of management in virtually every sphere dictates visitor behaviour to some degree. The extent to which a site appears cared for and to which the facilities provided on it are looked after will influence the manner in which the visitors treat them. So the attitude of management matters, and in the eyes of the visitor 'management' is not just the unseen administrator but is physically represented by every employee of the concern and of the concessionaires on the site. It matters, therefore, how the maintenance man behaves and how well or badly he does his job. The attitude of the canteen staff is taken, at any rate in part, as an indication of the attitude of the organization as a whole. The discourtesies of a badly run concession will be attributed by the public to the main enterprise in the same way as the pleasures afforded by any well-managed department within the whole. The price of success is eternal vigilance.

As mentioned above, in managing a recreational area, the attitude of management is all-important. Techniques used to control visitors will vary with the objectives of management. An area needing protection from the public will not be generally open to the public who may be excluded positively by physical barriers and warning notices (both of which draw attention to the existence of the protected area), or negatively by the simple process of 'hiding' the area, not calling attention to it by making access difficult or providing a strong counter-attraction.

One of the problems of control arises where management has an ambivalent attitude towards the visitor — as someone to be attracted in and provided for and at the same time, someone whose very presence causes disturbance to and degradation of the site and who ought, on those grounds, to be excluded. The on-site manager must in no way be uncertain about the attitude he should adopt, and the ultimate controller or owner must make his intentions clear, realizing however that the on-site management attitude may change from that of welcoming the visitor to that which over the years has become proprietorial with a duty it is to protect the area, its flora and fauna from the depredations of the now unwelcome public. Therefore, in devising methods of visitor control the 'marketing attitudes' of the proprietor will have to be taken into account.

Physical control presupposes some element of exclusion, and this may start off-site wich the negative-approach method of not advertising, or of restricting advertising, of diverting attention somewhere else, making access difficult or, indeed, imposing a charge, or higher charge, for entrance. On-site control is that which must be exercised to influence the behaviour of the visitor once he has arrived, and this may take many forms some of which have already been referred to above.

The site may be so laid out that the visitor, without his being aware of it, is directed along a particular path which itself is open and unfenced; one method of doing this is to allow grass to grow or gorse and bushes to flourish in some areas while elsewhere vegetation is cut short. Alternatively the visitor may be either excluded from an area or discouraged from entering it by permanent or temporary fencing; indeed, in some cases rough, easily climbable fencing may be successfully and deliberately used as a 'people-sifter', as may ditches or moats, stiles and kissing-gates all of which may, to a greater or lesser degree, discourage certain classes of visitor (e.g. the elderly or those already hampered by prams and push-chairs) while not positively prohibiting access to all.

Features and points of interest may be provided for the power which they have to draw visitors to them. They may be visible over a long distance or their hidden presence may be advertised. Although hardly points of special interest, lavatories, cafés and ice-cream stalls all have their devotees.

People tend to enjoy proprietorship and many may be expected to adopt a local park area as something special to themselves, and in the process become, in one way or another, protective towards it: they, and even strangers, may be encouraged into a sense of belonging by, for example, giving or adopting specific trees or shrubs.

Predominant, and often most misused, among control devices are the ubiquitous notices or other paraphernalia which convey messages from management to visitors, ranging from those which attempt to exercise positive authority to those giving information and advice. They may be categorized as follows:

(1) Notices which give orders usually with at least the implication of sanctions being taken against those who fail to obey (the 'Trespassers will be prosecuted' type of notice, most of which are in fact prohibitory). Too many of these notices may raise resentment and rebellion in the breast of even the most mild visitor.

(2) Notices which make requests but which neither threaten nor imply dire consequences if those requests are ignored.

(3) Notices which give information about the site or facilities or events of which visitors may take advantage or not as they please.

The information may be factual and straightforward or it may, on the other hand, be deliberate misinformation such as the now well-known 'Danger – adders' notice, or the more refined and meaningless 'Oxymoron and Anacoluthon set here: trespassers beware', which once enlivened the entrance to the grounds of a school. Sometimes while some inform-ation is given other information may be deliberately omitted (might this be termed zero information?), such as not referring to certain aspects of a site or leaving off a map certain places or facilities which in fact exist. Publicity notices may emphasize certain aspects of a site with the object of drawing people to them and thereby reducing pressures on other areas. Lastly there is the interpretive notice which is designed to educate rather than inform.

Notices themselves have a certain drawing power and may be used for this secondary purpose as well as for their prime purpose of ordering, requesting, informing or educating. A carefully sited notice can, therefore, be used to divert attention from something or draw attention to itself, thus to an extent diverting the visitor. The drawing power of a notice will tend to degrade the site on which it stands and management needs to be aware of this.

Monitoring visitor behaviour and visitor preferences must play an important part in the management of a recreational complex, for only by a knowledge of what visitors do, what they want and how they view the facilities provided can management tactics be devised and where necessary changed. Monitoring must be a two-way exercise as much concerned to find out how the running and presentation of the site strikes the visitor as to find out how the visitor treats the site. Visitor behaviour can be ascertained by observation and often the reasons for it by questioning; visitor preferences and the visitors' view of management can really only be measured by direct contact. Talking to or questioning visitors can, of course, be undertaken with the aid of preset questionnaire which, particularly where specific information is required, should prove satisfactory to management, though it is not always welcomed by those questioned. A general view of visitor-reaction, however, may be more satifactorily obtained by the apparently casual observer talking informally to groups of people as the opportunity arises, but here the preset questionnaire may not be particularly appropriate for it is often hard to anticipate the points which visitors may wish to express an opinion and visitors directly approached with a set of questions may not answer absolutely truthfully (possibly out of misplaced concern).

Formal, or apparently informal, monitoring by specially selected people is no doubt valuable. Equally valuable is the information collected daily by staff working on the site, who should be encouraged to regard this sort of monitoring as part of their normal duties – provided, of course, that they can be made to understand that they are not expected to carry out a sort of daily inquisition.

These methods of visitor monitoring require a degree of perception on the part of the observer or questioner as well as the observed or questioned, and an awareness on the part of the observer/questioner that this factor may lead to errors arising from ambiguous interpretation. There are, of course, methods of monitoring which rely on mechanical devices; cameras and metres measuring traffic flows are two obvious examples. The use of mechanical devices is also pertinent to monitoring in a different context, namely, monitoring the state of the site itself.

Financial monitoring is of primary importance in assessing commercial effectiveness and overall efficiency of management. The monitoring of visitor behaviour and visitor attitudes is also of paramount importance but and underlying assumption in both of these may be that the physical resources of the site remain unchanged. Use implies change and, although this change may be imperceptible in the short run, its existence is inevitable. For a variety of reasons resource changes may go unperceived by the manager: they may be so slow that recollection of original conditions may deteriorate as fast or faster than the resources themselves. A change in site manager may take with it any previous awareness of the changing condition of the site — the new manager implicitly tends to start his mental data-bank from the point at which he takes on the responsibility of management. No matter how slow or apparently imperceptible the change in natural site resources, it is likely to be far longer-lasting than the relatively transient changes in financial conditions or visitor behaviour.

We have seen how in adopting different criteria for assessing recreational carrying capacity a site manager may be relatively unconcerned with the deterioration of the natural elements of the site, preferring, for example, to replace them with less sensitive — even artificial — substitutes. However, the more directly concerned he becomes with countryside recreation, the more he is likely to be concerned also with resource conservation: it will increase in importance as an objective of management. But if management is to be explicitly assessed, mere acceptance of change does not negate the need to identify and measure changes which actually occur. This is the essence of monitoring.

We have already seen in Chapter 6 how site resources can be identified and evaluated. The extension of this appraisal process to form a basis for site monitoring is fairly apparent considering that identifying any deviation from the initial values is part of the monitoring function. Consequently the resource inventory which should exist for any operating enterprise is the most obvious starting-point for assessing the changing and shifting values of the natural resources of the site.

Monitoring is a relative process, its function being to chart patterns of change, and the first requirement for a monitoring system is a firm datum against which future change can be measured. Although the inventory goes a long way to providing a point of reference for future comparisons, it can only be expected to fulfil the task adequately if it has been prepared in the first instance with a view to filling this additional role. The most obvious 'extra' to be included with the resource inventory is a photographic record (with, of course, precise locations of each shot). The pictorial record can be easily updated from time to time — effectively producing a long-term time lapse sequence of photographs. Even the simplest visual record can be useful in identifying macrodeterioration of resources. More sophisticated variations such as infrared photography or the various techniques of aerial photography, though invariably evaluating the price of the information, may yield valuable additional information — still of a visual nature. For many monitoring systems this depth of information may be sufficient for management purposes, since monitoring itself is not synonymous with evaluation — simply with measurement of change.

The process of change extends beyond this visual level to changes in the ecosystems of the site. The site manager particularly concerned with ecological capacity will require information on the ecological change resulting from recreational use of the site. The monitoring of these changes follows the same principles, namely, to identify and carry out an initial evaluation of the resources and then to assess changes in those values. Again the importance of the original resource appraisal is apparent — it is difficult and costly to require of the monitoring system a greater degree of detail and analysis than that incorporated in the original appraisal. The primary variables influencing an ecosystem appear to be (a) species diversity, (b) uniqueness of classes of elements and (c) area.

In the instance when resource management assumes such a high priority in establishing management policy for the site, the site manager appointed is likely not only to be interested in natural history himself, but to have had some specific background training (whether it be academic or practical or both), enabling him to apply specialist expertise to recreational land management. In other circumstances, when for one reason or another a non-specialist site manager has none the less an interest in ecological/physical carrying capacity of the site, there are probably few areas related to his general expertise so richly served by dedicated and competent technical advice on questions concerning the monitoring of ecological changes. The manager's responsibility then becomes one of co-ordinating outside experts and above all of providing them with an adequate brief.

To find the answers to questions on the uniqueness, extent and diversity of species requires a high degree of technical competence, particularly when the questions may be related to such diverse topics as soil, water, vegetation, animal life, mineral features or archaeological remains. Similarly, expert external advice (if economically justifiable) may play an invaluable role in establishing an efficient resource monitoring system. In these circumstances the manager must ensure that the information delivered to him is presented in the form which will accord best with his own management requirements — he may be ready to admit to not having the specialist experience of an outside expert but, by the same token, he must not expect the same expert to be able to adopt the necessary land management perspective in presenting his expertise.

In all this there are two paramount considerations of which sight should never be lost, namely, the overall role of the monitoring system and the degree of flexibility which the system incorporates. Monitoring is not an end in itself, just one of the means enbling that end to be achieved. It is all too easy to establish a monitoring system which is simply an information dustbin — it goes in, is stored and may never see the light of day again. This is not only pointless, it is extremely wasteful of management resources. The information must be capable of almost automatically stimulating management action. It should invariably feed back to the primary operations of management — appraising objectives and policies, implementing any corrective action into the plan and imposing, if necessary, controls on future plans. If the manager is attentive to this role, he will be conscious of the need for either:

(a) maintaining continuity of response to monitored information;
or
(b) establishing performance thresholds which when exceeded will trigger appropriate management actions.

The former can be extremely expensive to maintain, while the latter presupposes the ability to predict future events. Often a newly established monitoring system may have to rely on continuous appraisal until action thresholds can be identified in the light of experience. Flexibility — the second prerequisite of an effective management system — must be present to enable the unforeseen circumstance or outcome to be incorporated in the overall functioning of management. Very often unforeseen events can be picked up most quickly by efficient monitoring. In fact, the most unforeseen events are likely to be the product of management activity itself — the laying out of a grass car park may cause more damage to the sward than a full season's operation. The very act of improving facilities may create considerable detrimental side-effects. Flexibility must not only extend to the fact of change itself, but also the conditions under which change occurs. To consider again the grass car park, erosion during long periods of dry weather may be insignificant in comparison with the damage which may occur during a short period of moderate usage during wet weather.

Monitoring may be viewed as the all-seeing, all-knowing heart of management, but although it is fundamentally important for effective management it can never be a substitute for management itself.

CHAPTER TEN

# *Interpretation*

The Oxford Dictionary defines *interpret* as to 'expound the meaning of' or to 'bring our the meaning of by artistic representation or performance'. Don Aldrige in his guide, *Principles of Countryside Interpretation and Interpretive Planning* (HMSO, 1975) points out that the interpretative centre, in the context of countryside interpretation, aims to communicate the significance of the site at which it is located. Countryside interpretation, therefore, seeks to expound the meaning or to communicate the significance of some aspect of an area which is on display and may indeed do so by artistic representation or performance.

Grant W. Sharpe, Professor of Outdoor Recreation, College of Forest Resources in the University of Washington, writes in Chapter 1, 'An overview of interpretation', in the book *Interpreting the Environment.*

Interpretation seeks to achieve three objectives. The first or primary objective ... is to assist the visitor in developing a keener awareness, appreciation and understanding of the area he ... is visiting . . . .

The second objective ... is to accomplish management goals. It can be done in two ways. First interpretation can encourage thoughtful use of the recreation resource on the part of the visitor ... second interpretation can be used to minimize human impact on the resource by guiding people away from fragile or overused areas . . . .

The third objective of interpretation is to promote public understanding of an agency and its programs. Every agency or corporation has a message to convey. Well-done interpretation favourably promotes the image of the agency which supplies it. If it is overdone, the message is labelled propaganda, rather than interpretation.

Not every country park, picnic site or long-distance footpath needs interpreting, but in the light of the fact that many people who visit the countryside know little about it and that many people who know the countryside would.like to know more, almost any degree of interpretation is likely to be appreciated. As the practice of countryside interpretation spreads the standards expected of it will grow, but this statement itself provides no answer about when it should actually be provided. The answer to the question 'When?' is subjective and dependent upon individual judgment, finance and the apparent demand of the visitor. There are, of course, some recreational situations where interpretation is unnecessary, for there is indeed nothing to interpret: one thinks, for example, of the 'fairground' type of provision; probably artificial, concerned with concentrated entertainment and in contrast to an area of quiet countryside available for peaceful enjoyment. Bearing in mind that most countryside visitors are urban dwellers an area of quiet, even if dramatic, countryside, almost certainly calls for interpretation of one kind or another, while the entertainment centre does not. But between these two extremes interpretation may well be called for whether it be interpretation of a human activity, of a building, of a way of life or of the countryside itself. A country park may be established in the grounds of an historic mansion whose gardens were designed in the Age of Elegance. It may also look out across the surrounding countryside. On the other hand, the park may itself be in an apparently wild area or formed out of old gravel pits, woodlands or mineral workings. Recreation may be found in the excitement of industrial archaeology or on footpaths in the high hills or on the waters of a new reservoir. In all of these cases, and indeed in many more, there lies scope for inspired interpretation. It must, however, be realized that the art of interpretation is not that of merely giving information, but of imaginatively collecting and processing facts so that the visitor becomes involved with the site, building or practice being described and is thus able to understand its significance.

Very few regions in the British Isles are truly 'natural'. The countryside has been made and fashioned by man, as has the urban and industrial landscape, and the moulding has been caused by economic and social forces, by the demand for the goods which man can produce and by the way in which the owners and occupiers of land have used it. Interpretation of any particular locality may describe the forces of change, geological, mechanical, economic and social, which have brought it to its present condition and show that those forces are still working. The area and its plant and animal wildlife have been produced under change, and under change they may disappear; thus, to a degree interpretation will teach the need for care and consideration. At this point it is worth remembering that effective interpretation may also be intended to have a contributory effect on this process of charge. Chapter 9 of this book deals with some measures of visitor control to which interpretation may be added as major tool in the hands of the recreational land manager. Interpretation is intended to promote understanding of the resource through which care and concern may be exercised, but it can also be presented in such a way as to focus attention in one direction and thus away from another.

Each place, each thing displayed, has its own unique quality and, while there are interpretative ground-rules which can be applied generally, each problem is as unique as its subject and so is its solution. Nevertheless one of the basic tenets of interpretation is that it must be founded on an inherently sound understanding of the subject material. Research is the foundation of effective interpretation — and, moreover, research of both subject and object. Research into the material being interpreted is readily accepted but what is so often overlooked is that, if the message is never absorbed by the intended audience, its presentation simply represents wasted effort — effective interpretation requires effective communication. The message must be appropriate to the subject and audience and the conditions under which it is to be delivered.

Interpretation is not exactly synonymous with education, for it can do little more than scratch the surface of truth, yet it will certainly have achieved its aim if it awakens the interest and desire of the visitor to know more. But more about what? In the context of recreational land management interpretation is normally referred to in a site-specific sense; it is usually related, fairly directly, to its physical location somehow or other. We are, in fact, talking about a specific facet of interpretation. Arguably, it may be more effectively exploited not by reference to its own location but, for example, by reference to the audience with whom it is attempting to communicate. Some of the public information films shown on television provide an excellent example of the latter approach: the power and variability of the medium enables the message to be conveyed without necessarily placing any reliance on a specific location.

In a different way interpretation through the media of displays and exhibitions may be most effectively undertaken within an urban environment because of the nature of the subject material or access to a wider audience. The power of interpretation in a much broader environmental sense than exists in Britain is found in France where, for example, in major urban-development schemes such as La Défense in Paris, imaginative audiovisual programmes explain the purpose and progress of the development. Conversely displays which are normally associated with a relatively urban setting – those, for example, of the larger municipal museums – may be substantially enhanced when immersed in the country side: the Netherlands Kröllemuller Museum, with its internationally re-nowned display of fine art, is located in the tranquil and inspiring sur-roundings of the Hocht Velluwe National Park.

When considering interpretation as expounding a meaning in isolation from the reality, the possible variations are numerous. Similarly we find numerous permutations in considering the more specific role of inter-pretation in recreational land management, ranging from displays in visitor and information centres to the entertaining diversions of lions on show in an English park. Interpretation implies judgment of what is 'good' and 'bad' in a variety of circumstances. Selectivity is most import-ant, so where interpretation is likely to figure in the development and management of a site for recreation it should be afforded the same planne and systematic treatment as any other component of the overall manage-ment plan.

Interpretation is not an exercise which can be effectively undertaken by somebody who knows nothing about it. This may appear so simple a statement as to be unnecessary, but it is surprising to what extent inter-pretative duties are allocated by management to a member of the manage-ment team as a part, and perhaps a minor part, of his work. This may be acceptable if, in fact, the intention is not really to interpret but to inform (but even then the provision of acceptable information is not something to be undertaken lightly by a person busy with another job). Where, however, interpretation is to be undertaken seriously, it will have to be done by specialists and co-ordinated by an expert. Interpretative planning is, indeed, a part of the work of the management team and will need to progress by logical steps from formulation to implementation and thence to monitoring.

Clarity of objective is of paramount importance to the interpretative plan for two reasons, one related to utility and the other to effective implementation. The importance of interpretation as a management tool is well recognized: there is, however, the possibility that it may be oversimply viewed as just one more technique in the manager's box of tricks. Interpretation has its own particular ethic, and while this may be upheld by the manager it may differ from the management objectives for the enterprise as a whole. An association of ideas may plausibly link the notions of influencing the behaviour and attitudes of visitors through interpretation – particularly when emphasis is placed on the evangelizing role of interpretation – and influencing them through advertising. This can only result in a debasement of the philosophy of interpretation. Interpretation is only as effective as the chain of communication via the chosen media to the chosen audience. People are the benefactors of interpretation and they must always be at the forefront of the interpreter's mind. Otherwise it may easily fall short of its potential for enhancing visitor experience for a variety of reasons but particularly those arising from a misallocation of effort.

In the first instance the objectives of interpretation on the site need to be agreed, because only when this is done can any worthwhile consideration be given to what and how to interpret. With the ordering of the objective must be included the identification of constraints which, at this stage, may be largely financial, but which may also take the form of certain specific instructions such, for example, that it is not the intention to provide an interpretative centre or, indeed, that it is. The objectives having been specified and the constraints identified, the interpretative planner may then proceed to the next step: the selection of those items which appear to be suitable subjects for interpretation. This may involve the employment of specialists capable of investigating specific areas (e.g. botanists, archaeologists) and researchers who can work under their direction. The material thus collected will have to be evaluated and sifted and a first choice made of the subjects to be taken further. It is possible that at this stage with the amount of information available, a revision or modification of the original objectives may be necessary — even to the extent of discussing a possible change in the original constraints. A plan may emerge which will enumerate the subjects to be interpreted and put forward a number of choices or mixes from which the decision-maker may select a programme.

At this point a first discussion of the interpretative media to be used and of the cost may take place. The adoption of a reasonably firm plan is now feasible which can be worked up and priced in detail. The final stages pass through the adoption of the plan to its implementation. Interpretation however is never complete, for the implemented plan must be subsequently monitored so that management is made continually aware of visitor reaction to it and enabled thereby to introduce considered changes if necessary. These changes may be such as to alter objectives or the items to be interpreted or the method of interpretation employed, thus the interpretative process continues (see Fig. 17).

Interpretation is a very human process but although it is often carried out on a person-to-person basis (guided tours, for example) it may also be achieved through impersonal media (scientific displays, etc.). In many

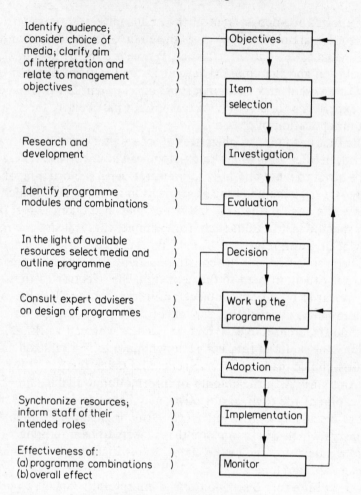

Identify audience;
consider choice of
media; clarify aim
of interpretation and
relate to management
objectives

Research and
development

Identify programme
modules and combinations

In the light of available
resources select media and
outline programme

Consult expert advisers
on design of programmes

Synchronize resources;
inform staff of their
intended roles

Effectiveness of:
(a) programme combinations
(b) overall effect

Objectives

Item
selection

Investigation

Evaluation

Decision

Work up the
programme

Adoption

Implementation

Monitor

Fig. 17 Planning for interpretation

instances personal media may be inappropriate — the cost effectiveness
of guided tours for small numbers of visitors may be questionable — and
the communicative effectiveness of the interpreter conveying the same
simple message to a continually changing audience may diminish as the
day wears on and the enthusiasm of the interpreter flags. Obviously the
decision to adopt personal/impersonal techniques will vary with changing circumstances and from site to site.

If the area warrants it, and if finance permits, the visitor on arrival
may be channelled through an interpretative exhibit which will tell him
something about what he is going to see. It may describe by pictures,

models, maps and in writing, the geology, land form, flora and fauna of
the area. It may trace the history of a building or a family or a way of
life. It may personalize the story, relating events as they affected an
individual or a group or an animal species. To be effective, however, the
exhibit should be vivid, eye-catching and not too big. Descriptive signs
or notices should be as short as possible, for the public is disinclined to
linger to read, and in any event too wordy a notice, if read, will cause an
irritating hold up in the flow of visitors; and if not read, might as well
not have been written. Ideally the exhibit should be explicit enough for
the visitor to understand its impact quickly and small or brief enough to
linger in his memory. Afterwards he goes outside to study more closely
what he may have come to see, or what he now should want to see, with
wider understanding. The interpretation, then, will have influenced the
visitor in at least three ways: giving him a sharpened awareness; awaken-
ing a real desire to look at particular features in the area; and so concentrating his interest in one sphere that it is diverted from others which
need protection.

It can be tempting to tell the visitor too much and perhaps show him
things which are not relative to the site but of supreme interest to the
person staging the display. Where plans for an exhibit in a visitor centre
veer towards, or indeed take on the form of, a countryside museum or
other absorbing display unrelated to the site, management should be
prepared to ask again what is the aim of the display before sanctioning it.
This is not to say that unrelated exhibitions should always be banned,
they may have great drawing-power and be all-absorbing, but equally
well they might have been mounted elsewhere leaving room for the
practice of interpretation to be carried on where it has relevance, namely,
where its subject lies.

Interpretation is not solely confined to the display in a visitor centre:
it may be simply a notice describing a function or process, scene or
event on the ground. The scene itself is there, it has no need to be
reproduced to be explained. Sometimes, of course, explanation is
difficult if not impossible. The weaving process, or even the progress of
a cow through the milking-parlour, is more easily understood if it happens
before the visitor's eye than if the machinery is static and the essential
movement frozen into cold print: besides, a notice cannot be plied with
questions and this is where the guide-interpreter may, in a given instance,
be the ideal medium. Such a person must himself fully understand what
it is he is interpreting. An ill-informed guide is often worse than no guide
at all.

Many visitor-centres now have a small auditorium where films, or more often slides, can be shown on topics connected with the site. The prepared slide programme is linked to a tape-recorded running commentary and the combined performance can be very effective. It is easy to be critical and to wonder sometimes how far interpretation can or should be taken before, as mentioned earlier, it becomes the equivalent of an off-site exhibition. It should then be asked whether the programme could not better be provided in the town or on the urban-fringe site, where more people could see it and where perhaps it could be extended into the educational sphere and be readily available all the year round. There is no certain answer to this uncertain question, but the question should be posed nevertheless, for it relates to the answer to the planner's problem: 'What, on this site, am I seeking to interpret and why?'

It is easy for the enthusiast to get carried away and, in the process, begin to educate rather than interpret or stage an exhibition which is too sophisticated. He must never forget to consider the sort of visitor to whom he is addressing himself, among whom will be many of the impatient young and some of the defective elderly (who move slowly and whose senses may have become dulled). People, old or young, like to touch and feel things and the provision of tangible objects, polished stone or wood, will give satisfaction and deepen awareness: in the young the desire to learn through the sense of touch is strong and often express-ed by an inability to leave things alone, hence the need to put out of reach things which children are likely to grab, overwork, pick up, eat or otherwise destroy.

If a visitor centre is to be provided, care should be taken to decide what it is going to contain before the final design is agreed. The intention may be, for example, to provide information and interpretation, a café and lavatories and, within the interpretation section, an exhibition and perhaps an auditorium. Auditorium, lavatories, information desk, café and exhibition must be sited with an awareness of who is going to use them, when and how, so that as far as possible a confusion of visitors and cross-traffic is avoided. It may, indeed, be better to physically separate interpretation from information and from the mundane facilities of lavatories and tea. This leads one to ask at what stage in a visit interpretation is most required.

The theme of this chapter so far has been to the effect that inter-pretation should be designed to explain and to expound the meaning of something, and through this function to awake the visitor's understanding before he goes out on to the site. This surely must be right. There remains the fact that questions are often asked at the end of a visit and as a result of it, and the possibility that they might be answered by an informative and interpretative exhibition through which departing visitors could be channelled. Their many and varied questions are probably better dealt with through the medium of personal contact with members of staff whose reporting of the questions asked of them should be treated as a form of monitoring of the adequacy or inadequacy of the interpretation and information already provided.

There remains also to be mentioned the least of interpretation techniques, namely, the self-guided tour which may be undertaken with the aid of a descriptive handout, along a marked trail, with recognized stopping-places, where interpretation may be enhanced by permanent notices. While this can be termed the 'least' of interpretation techniques, it is not on that account necessarily simple in execution, for the preparation of the handout, the laying out and marking of a route and the composition of interpretative notices need careful and knowledgeable thought.

The success of any interprative medium lies not in the expertise with which it appears to be handled nor necessarily in the delight with which it may be welcomed by a specialist section of the public, but in the degree of interest which it arouses in the general run of visitors. This will be gauged only by monitoring, to which reference has already been made.

In earlier chapters of this book mention has been made of the selection of enterprises, of building a management model and of the preparation of a management plan; a part of that plan may make reference to interpretation but it is unlikely that any details of the process will be given at that early stage. Indeed, interpretation needs separate consideration and a separate plan which is probably best thought about apart from, but never in isolation from, the management plan itself. Reference was also made to the selection of enterprise and attention drawn to the possibility of starting the process by eliminating from a checklist those which were clearly impossible and those which were incompatible with the site or with each other. It could be that the interpretation plan might be compiled in a like manner not by writing down a prearranged list and then applying it to the site, but by compiling a list of subjects appropriate to the site and afterwards eliminating those which for one reason or another should not be proceeded with. In compiling the list it may be helpful to do so under a number of headings such as: archaeology, architecture, geology, geography, biology, ecology, history, industry, transportation and communication. Each of these may be divided into a number of subheadings and consideration given to them. For example:

*Geology* being the science of the composition, history and structure of the earth's crust and

*Physical geography*, being the science of describing the earth's surface or physical features of the surface, would combined, produce a study of the structure and appearance of the landscape.

*Biology*, being the study of living organisms, would produce a study of plants, insects, birds and animals on the site and

*Ecology* (land-based or water-based) would provide a study of the relations of living organisms to their environment. Included in this particular study could be the effect of the opening up of the site to the public on these living organisms, and indeed upon the appearance of the site, thus linking the biological study with those under the geological and geographical headings.

*History* would bring in consideration of man's use of the site and its particular importance in the interpretative context. Events which may have taken place in or near the area and which are a part of the nation's history are, of course, important, but it should be remembered that a study of history does not have to be confined to widely known happenings, for the personal history of individuals, families, or the local population, can often form fascinating stories as can an imaginatively presented review of a past way of life.

*Archaeology* might properly be classified as a subheading of History but is so important on certain sites that it is certainly worth mentioning separately here.

*Architecture* could stand on its own, or indeed be omitted from the general list, because in its concern which design and workmanship, it is so obviously appropriate in the specific case where a building is the main attraction or an integral part of the site.

*Industry* entails thought about what man produced or produces on or outside the site and would include, of course, the use of land for agriculture and forestry as well as for the manufacturing or extractive industries.

*Transportation and communication* would consider old and new roads and tracks through the area as well as any other significant methods of transport (e.g. railways) and methods of communication (e.g. telegraphs) for which part of the site may be, or have been, used.

The number of headings could, no doubt, be increased, but it is suggested that the main areas of investigation are covered by those set out here. On any single site, there may be nothing to note under several of the headings, nor, if there is an entry under a particular heading, is there any certainty that the matter is worth pursuing. At the very least consideration of these headings should enable those facets of the area which are susceptible to interpretation to be identified and an ordered list of possibilities prepared; priorities can then be allocated to these. To a degree these priorities may be judged on a practical basis such as, for example, the cost of further investigation and of interpreting the findings; but to a further degree judgment is almost bound to be subjective and dependent upon the assessor's personal interests and his determination of the amount of public interest likely to be aroused by the various possibilities.

# Index